The Biology of Human Communication

Second Edition

Kory Floyd, Arizona State University

Contributing Authors:
Alan C. Mikkelson, Whitworth College
Colin Hesse, Arizona State University

Australia • Brazil • Japan • Korea • Mexico • Singapore • Spain • United Kingdom • United States

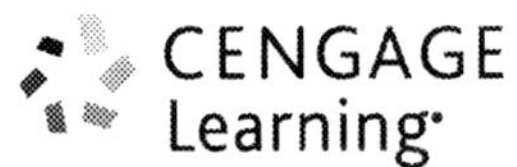

The Biology of Human Communication: Second Edition
Kory Floyd, Arizona State University

Executive Editors:
Maureen Staudt
Michael Stranz

Senior Project Development Manager:
Linda deStefano

Marketing Specialist:
Courtney Sheldon

Senior Production/Manufacturing Manager:
Donna M. Brown

PreMedia Manager:
Joel Brennecke

Sr. Rights Acquisition Account Manager:
Todd Osborne

Cover Image:
Getty Images*

*Unless otherwise noted, all cover images used by Custom Solutions, a part of Cengage Learning, have been supplied courtesy of Getty Images with the exception of the Earthview cover image, which has been supplied by the National Aeronautics and Space Administration (NASA).

For product information and technology assistance, contact us at
Cengage Learning Customer & Sales Support, 1-800-354-9706
For permission to use material from this text or product,
submit all requests online at **cengage.com/permissions**
Further permissions questions can be emailed to
permissionrequest@cengage.com

ISBN-13: 978-1-4266-2676-0

ISBN-10: 1-4266-2676-2

Cengage Learning
5191 Natorp Boulevard
Mason, Ohio 45040
USA

Cengage Learning is a leading provider of customized learning solutions with office locations around the globe, including Singapore, the United Kingdom, Australia, Mexico, Brazil, and Japan. Locate your local office at:
international.cengage.com/region.
Cengage Learning products are represented in Canada by Nelson Education, Ltd.
For your lifelong learning solutions, visit **custom.cengage.com.**
Visit our corporate website at **cengage.com.**

Printed in the United States of America

Contents

Chapter One: Introduction

Paul and Adam became best friends in the third grade. Their families lived not far from each other, and they often spent time together on the weekends and over school vacations. They were inseparable all the way through junior high and high school. They both started on the school's basketball team, they learned how to drive together, and as they approached graduation, they decided to room together when they headed to college.

It was late in the fall semester of their freshman year in college when they both met Shelley. She was cute and flirtatious and lived a few floors up from Paul and Adam in the same residence hall. Adam was smitten immediately. He started making excuses just to go up to Shelley's floor, on the chance that he might run into her. He found that he couldn't stop thinking about her; when they were together, he felt overwhelmed with excitement, and when they were apart, he couldn't seem to focus on anything else. Adam's grades started to slip as he turned in assignments late (or not at all), and Paul noticed that Adam was having trouble sleeping. For the first time in his life, Adam was head-over-heels in love.

The problem was, Shelley liked Paul instead. She thought Adam was cute and funny and a kick to be around, but she often agreed to spend time with him only as a means of getting access to Paul. Paul didn't share her feelings – he had his eye on someone from his geology class – but Shelley decided to get bold one night and tell Paul how she felt about him. When Adam got word of this, he felt completely crushed. It was like someone had kicked him in the gut. Even though he knew that Paul wasn't interested in Shelley, finding out that Shelley was interested in Paul, and not him, was a huge blow to his ego and self-confidence. After being on a constant high for several weeks, Adam sank into a deep depression. He barely ate and he sometimes slept 12 to 14 hours a day. He became withdrawn from others, and sadly, his friendship with Paul suffered as well. At the end of their freshman year, Paul decided to move to an apartment off campus, and Adam continued to struggle with school for some time afterward.

Relationships are challenging, and communicating within our relationships can seem, at times, to be especially daunting. It's tough to tell people how we feel about them sometimes, and it can be even tougher when they don't feel the same way about us. Maybe you've been through something very similar to what Adam, Shelley, or Paul experienced; if so, then you know first-hand how easily we can get caught up in the emotion that goes along with relational communication.

As the example illustrates, however, it's not just our thoughts and feelings that are affected by the communication in our relationships. Our bodies are intricately involved, as well. Take Adam, for example. When he was madly in love, he had intense feelings of excitement when he was around Shelley, and feelings of restlessness when he wasn't. He found it hard to focus and hard to sleep. By contrast, when Shelley professed her attraction to Paul, Adam's body felt like it shut down. He couldn't eat, he couldn't smile, and many other things in his life, including his grades, his friendships, and his relationship with Paul, suffered as a result. The point is, Adam didn't experience his attraction to Shelley, and his rejection from her, in purely mental, emotional, or intellectual ways. These were very physical experiences as well. In turn, these physical reactions affected how he interacted with the other important people in his life.

This is a book about the relationship between biology and human communication. We may not think about it very often, but our bodies are constantly engaged in shaping and coloring our communication with others – and our communication, in turn, affects how well our bodies work. We will explore many of the ways in which people experience this biology-communication connection in this text.

To prime our discussion, we have chosen to begin by explaining what it means to take a biological approach to studying communication. Afterward, we will give you an introduction to the scientific method and describe some of the ways science can help us to understand human behavior. Both of these prefaces will give you important frameworks for understanding the information we present in the body of this book. We will close this chapter with a brief overview of the text. We hope that our discussion here will help you to understand, and to appreciate, the myriad ways in which our bodies and our behaviors work together everyday.

What does Biology have to do with Communication?

Think about the last time you got into a really heated argument with someone. Do you remember how you felt? Did your heart beat faster? Did it feel like your blood pressure was going up? Maybe you got that tight feeling in your chest, and it felt like your breathing became heavier or more labored. Could you feel your hands trembling? Perhaps you even got to the point when you simply couldn't say anything more.

Now, think about the most romantic experience you've ever had. Maybe it was on a first date, or perhaps it was with a long-time romantic partner. Think about how it felt when you looked into each other's eyes, when you touched, when you kissed. Remember the shiver you felt as the hairs on your neck stood on end. Remember feeling your pulse race and your body getting warmer. Perhaps you can even remember having feelings of sexual arousal.

These are just two of many examples of how biology and communication are intertwined. We humans are built for social interaction – it is our way of being, our *raison d'être.* But it's more than just our minds, our personalities, and our souls that are involved in the communication process – our bodies are fully engaged as well. With our ears, we hear the cries of our children and the voices of our adversaries. With our eyes, we observe facial expressions and evaluate personal appearance. With our mouths, we speak, we sing, we celebrate and whine and yell and congratulate. With our arms, we hold our loved ones tight and push others away from us. With our bodies, we grieve and rejoice, we make war and we make love.

The truth is, *nothing* about human communication is divorced from biology: our brains conceive of it and our bodies produce and react to it. Without biology, you wouldn't have the ability to read this book and we wouldn't have had the ability to write it. There would be no great speeches to study, no performances to analyze, no relationships to examine. Communication isn't a living, breathing thing that exists on its own; it requires humans, who are biological creatures, in order to exist. And humans, like most living creatures, are well adapted to the needs of their communicative environments.

Consider the argument and the romantic exchange we asked you to recall above. You might have noticed, as you thought about each experience, that your physical response was somewhat the same in both situations: your heart rate and blood pressure went up, your breathing rate and body temperature rose, you sweated more, and perhaps you trembled. Now, of course, your mental and emotional experiences in the two situations were probably very different, but your body responded in quite similar ways. Why? Because, in both situations, you needed more energy than normal. To provide you with that extra energy, your heart beat faster so that your blood could carry more oxygen to your organs and muscles. This caused your blood pressure to increase as well. In addition, you began to breathe more heavily in order to take in more oxygen. Your body temperature went up because of this arousal you were feeling, and you sweated more in order to keep yourself from overheating. And, some of that excess energy probably spilled out of your body in the form of shaking or trembling.

Many other things were happening, too, that you may have had less awareness of. In the argument, your hypothalamus, pituitary, and adrenal glands produced stress hormones. These caused your blood to convert more glucose to sugar for excess energy. Meanwhile, energy was being diverted away from your digestive and reproductive systems. Your pupils dilated and your rate of metabolism changed temporarily. In the romantic exchange, your body produced hormones called dopamine, oxytocin, and endorphins, which gave you that warm, glowing feeling. The capillaries near the surface of your skin expanded, making your skin temperature rise. If the situation progressed to a sexual encounter, your pupils dilated, your lips became engorged, and your reproductive organs became aroused.

This book is about these types of connections between your communication activities and your biological and physiological processes. Communication engages many of our bodily systems, sometimes in similar ways and sometimes in different ways. To understand how, it is first necessary for you to have some background knowledge about how your various bodily systems work. Afterward, you can apply what you know to the task of understanding various communicative contexts, such as conflict, attraction, stress, parenting, and the like.

Before we address the specifics of the biology of communication further, let us first discuss what it does and does not mean to take a biological approach to the study of communication. Many people in the academic community (and many in the communication discipline, specifically) deride such an approach, either out of the belief that all communication behavior is socially or culturally learned, or out of discomfort at what a biological approach to human behavior implies. So that you don't have to struggle with either type of issue, we want to directly address these concerns and explain why communication students and researchers needn't shy away from trying to understand *how communication and biology are intertwined.* After all, just thinking about an argument or a romantic episode ought to have been enough to convince you that they are.

We want to address the second issue first – that is, discomfort with some of the supposed implications of a biological approach. We call the implications *supposed* because, in fact, the biological approach does not imply any of them. There are three, in particular, we wish to discuss: the **deterministic fallacy**, the **immutability fallacy**, and the **naturalistic fallacy**. We will address the first two together.

Determinism and Immutability

When they hear that behavior might be related to biology, many people jump to the conclusion that biology *determines* behavior. This conclusion seems to suggest that people have no control over their behaviors, and that environmental influences such as our culture, our education, or the way we raise our children, are meaningless. Because this idea seems so undesirable, and so counter to their lived experience, many people are led to reject the idea that biology has anything to do with behavior.

In point of fact, however, the conclusion was false to begin with. To say that biology and communication are related is not to say that biology determines behavior. This erroneous conclusion is called the deterministic fallacy. Now, a clarification is in order: as we noted before, our biology gives us the *ability* to communicate. This is evidenced most clearly in cases when people are biologically constrained in some way, such as those born blind or deaf. People with vision or hearing loss must adopt alternative ways of communicating to compensate for biological abilities that others may take for granted. However, the ability to communicate does not dictate the *manner* in which we communicate, any more than the ability to write dictates the words we use or the ability to sing dictates the songs we enjoy.

Besides making environmental influences seem irrelevant, the idea of determinism would also seem to suggest that we have no control over our behavior: our biology makes us do what it will, and we can neither control nor change it. This is the idea behind the immutability fallacy, and it, too, is a misunderstanding of the biological approach. To say that something is related to biology in no way implies that it cannot be controlled or changed. Personality traits, such as how shy or argumentative you are, appear to be largely inherited genetically (e.g., Beatty, Heisel, Hall, Levine, & La France, 2002; Beatty, Marshall, & Rudd, 2001), yet with education and experience, people can learn to control their propensities for argument or change their tendencies to shy away from social interaction (we can all think of shy people who "opened up" with experience in a new situation). Much as we may wish to defend our behavior by saying "my genes made me do it," the reality is that our biology simply *predisposes us* toward certain behaviors. We still have control over, and responsibility for, how we act.

The Naturalistic Fallacy

Here's another misunderstanding that causes people to reject a biological influence on behavior: to call something *natural* is tantamount to endorsing it morally. That is, if we say that a certain predisposition, such as a predisposition for aggression, has biological (or natural) roots, that's like saying it's morally okay. A notable example comes from a book by Thornhill and Palmer (2002) in which the authors argued that, contrary to our cultural and political notions, rape is not about power and control but is simply an evolved adaptation that works to increase men's chances for reproduction. As you might imagine, many took immediate offense to this idea, believing that the authors were arguing that since rape was adaptive, then they must believe it to be morally acceptable and excusable. In fact, the authors argued no such thing; they believe, as we do, that rapists must be held accountable for their destructive behavior. However, they argued that as long as scientists turn a blind eye toward the sexual drives motivating men to rape, their efforts to reduce instances of rape would be destined to fail.

This idea – the naturalistic fallacy – is also a misunderstanding of the biological approach. Identifying the biological roots of a behavior or behavioral tendency has absolutely nothing to do with passing moral judgment on it. The misguided logic that gives rise to this fallacy is this: since we have no control over our biological make-up, whatever is biologically based must be *good*. Well, there can be little question that the sex drive is biologically based, but we all know that some sex acts are morally sanctioned and others are not. By the same token, finding out that something we thought was a learned behavior actually has biological roots doesn't imply that it should be any more or less morally acceptable than it was before. There simply is no logical link between the two. When researchers work to understand the cause of some behavior (even if that cause is biological), that doesn't imply anything about their moral acceptance of that behavior.

Even if they understand these three fallacies – the deterministic, immutability, and naturalistic fallacies – some people are still inclined to dismiss the idea that human behavior could have biological roots because that seems to negate the importance of learning, culture, socialization, and upbringing. We'll address this in the next section.

What about Learning?

When you think about it, enculturation, socialization, and upbringing (how you were raised and nurtured by your parents) are all forms of *learning*. We learn the ideas and practices of our culture; they are not imprinted on us at birth. As we are socialized and brought up, our various sources of influence (parents, teachers, friends, the media) affect us through learning: we see, or are told, what is proper and what is not. As a result, we will use the term *learning* to refer to all of these various influences.

You've probably heard of the "nature vs. nurture" debate many times. If so, it may have been explained to you as the clash between the idea that human behavior is dictated by biology (the *nature* side) and the idea that it is dictated by learning (in all its forms; the *nurture* side). At the heart of this debate is the question of whether humans are born as "blank slates," ready to be imprinted upon by their parents, teachers, cultural traditions, and other such influences, or whether humans are both with particular personalities and dispositions that are genetically grounded, not learned. Perhaps you've thought about this question yourself, and perhaps you even know which side of the debate seems more sensible to you.

We're going to suggest here that the nature-nurture debate is largely a pointless, illogical one. We believe it creates a false dichotomy to suggest that the cause of a behavior is *either* nature *or* nurture (which one does by thinking of them as opposing forces). Nearly every behavior of interest to communication researchers can reasonably be said to have some measure of biological influence *and* some measure of learned influence. You should understand that we're not saying this as a cop-out to evade the debate. Not all dichotomies (this vs. that) are false ones, and just because two ideas are in opposition to one another, that doesn't necessarily mean that the truth lies somewhere in between. Sometimes one idea is just *right* and the other is *wrong*...but this is not one of those times. The nature-nurture debate obscures the fact that biology and learning interact in complex ways and that some biological predispositions can only influence behavior under certain learned conditions. Let's say that your neurological structure gives you a particular capacity for learning languages. That's great – but you still have to learn the languages before you can speak them. That is, your biologically driven capacity won't influence your behavior unless you learn what you need to learn.

Most important to note, however, is that biology and learning are not on equal footing with each other, but are hierarchically ordered. The very ability to learn is, in itself, biological. If people don't have the neurological and physiological capacity to learn in the first place, then their socialization, culture, and upbringing won't have any effect on them. By contrast, biology can affect behavior in the absence of learning. Anyone who has had children knows this: newborn babies haven't learned, for instance, the culturally appropriate means of expressing their emotions. Their behaviors are driven by biological needs: their need for food, for warmth, for safety and quiet. If babies didn't have a biologically grounded capacity to learn, then they would continue acting like babies for the remainder of their lives.

What should we conclude about learning, then? It is extremely important, and no social scientist worth his or her salt would say otherwise. We humans learn our languages, we learn how to run our lives, and we learn how to co-exist, how to dominate, how to pair bond, and how to raise our young. We learn how to do our jobs and fold our clothes, balance our checkbooks and drive our cars and plan our vacations. We don't come out of the womb with any of this information – we have to learn it all through observation, through direct education, through our cultural and social and political messages, through our socialization as human beings. We learn some of these things better than others, and this helps to make us individuals and to define who is *like* us and who is *unlike* us. All of this makes it possible for researchers, educators, and advertisers to craft images, messages, and stories to inform, persuade, and entertain us. Learning is, in no way, an explanation for human behavior that opposes biology – the more accurate view is that learning works *through biology.*

Having said all of this, we suspect that the importance of studying biological influences on communication behavior is becoming clear, and that's our mission in this book. If we are truly to understand how biology affects our behavior, and how our behavior affects our biological processes, it's important that we know something about the scientific method, in which the research we review in this book has been conducted. You probably already know that there are several ways to study human communication. Some researchers use ethnography to understand people's constructions of ideas by become embedded within their social groups. Some use rhetorical criticism to explicate and provide perspective on arguments in spoken and written messages. The research we describe in this book has been conducted using the scientific method, which is unique among approaches for studying communication. We'll explain how in the next section.

Taking a Scientific Approach to Studying Communication

We all know what science is. It's the study of things in test tubes, right? It's the dissection of frogs or the exploration of outer space. If you were asked to think of a scientist, chances are you'd conjure up an image of a person in a white lab coat, working with bubbling flasks in a laboratory or leading little white mice through a maze. Given this concept of science, and of scientists, it's not difficult to see why so many people have a hard time understanding how one can study human communication scientifically. How will they fit people into those little test tubes?

In truth, science is not a *topic* of study; it's a *method* of study. Anything in the physical universe – and that includes people – can be studied using the scientific method. And anyone who employs the scientific method in his or her research is, by definition, a scientist, white lab coat or not. To a scientist, human behavior is no different than the behavior of photons, the behavior of plants, or the behavior of asteroids, insofar as it is occurring within the physical universe and can therefore be studied using the principles of science.

No different than the behavior of photons? Do scientists see humans as faceless, mindless machines, who all act in the same way under the same circumstances? What about individuality? Culture? Free will? The fact that nobody else is exactly like me? Don't these things make it impossible to study human behavior scientifically? Not in the slightest. Very few things that scientists study are all exactly alike: plants aren't, animals aren't, stars and amoebas and rocks aren't. Variety is the spice of scientific life, too; what science looks for are meaningful ways to explain those differences. In fact, medical science has long been conducted on humans – individual though they are – to advance understanding of the body and to contribute to the creation of treatments and medicines that improve the quality of our lives.

Yes, you might say, *but studying the body is one thing; physically, we're all pretty much the same. That's not true of communication behavior.* You're right. But the communication scientist isn't trying to find things that are true of all people all of the time. We're still individuals, and we still have the ability to act in unexpected ways. The scientist tries to discover what is true of *most people most of the time.* What persuasive techniques are the most effective in getting people to wear their seatbelts? What methods of teaching are the most effective in helping students to learn difficult material? What styles of managing conflict are the most likely to help marriages succeed? Even though each of us is an individual, scientists can still uncover patterns in our behavior – they may not explain every single situation, but they can explain most situations most of the time.

To understand the scientific method, one needs to begin by thinking about the nature of knowledge. What does it mean to *know* something? This is the principal question in the field of philosophy known as **epistemology**, and it can be answered in several different ways. We know some things because of intuition. Maybe you're in a particular situation and you *just know* that something is wrong; you sense that you're in danger, for instance, and so you leave. We know other things because of our personal experience. For example, you might know that, when you need money, it's better to ask your dad than your mom because your experience tells you that you'll be more successful taking that approach. Still other things we know because of authority: someone who ought to know told us. A doctor, a teacher, or the Internet gives us certain information, and because we trust that the source is credible, we believe the information. Most religious knowledge is of this type: we know that certain actions are right and others are wrong because an authority (a minister, the Bible, the Pope) said so.

Intuition, personal experience, and authority are all powerful ways of knowing, insofar as humans rely on them to make decisions about their lives. In fact, we often prefer these ways of knowing over scientific knowledge – perhaps you can recall a time when you've heard a "scientific fact," only to dismiss it because, say, your personal experience told you otherwise. For example, if you've ever taken a course in interpersonal or nonverbal communication, perhaps you've been taught that, contrary to the stereotype, *men are actually more talkative than women* (Mulac, 1989). Come again? If you're like many students, you find that hard to believe because your personal experience tells you different – we can all think of men who never seem to talk and women who never seem to stop.

This is a good example, though, of the problem with knowledge that comes from intuition, personal experience, and even authority: it is quite often *wrong*. That doesn't mean people don't trust these types of knowledge; it means that the "knowledge" may not be accurate. Perhaps you would've bet $100 that women are more talkative than men, because *everybody knows that.* You can kiss your hundred bucks goodbye.

Why are these types of knowledge so prone to being wrong? Perhaps the biggest reason is that we don't subject them to very much scrutiny. Let's take an example from medicine: praying for sick people helps them heal. Some people would say they know this because of authority – a religious text or a religious figure told them so, and they believed it. Others, however, would say that they know it from personal experience; perhaps they had a sick grandmother whom they prayed for, and she recovered. *I know it's true because I've seen it happen,* someone might say.

Now, prayer may very well aid the healing process (we'll examine some evidence later in this chapter). We're certainly not suggesting that just because something is known by intuition, experience, or authority, it is necessarily wrong – on the contrary, such knowledge is often accurate. Before you wager another $100, though, consider this: most medical problems resolve themselves. The body has amazing healing capacities. So, does the fact that you prayed for your grandmother and she recovered *prove* that prayer aids healing? How about if 1,000 people prayed for their sick relatives, and they all recovered? Would this be enough evidence to prove that prayer aids healing?

The answer, from the scientific perspective, is no. As a fourth way of knowing (besides intuition, personal experience, and authority), science demands a much greater degree of scrutiny. We'll return to the prayer example in a moment – first, let us explore what makes the scientific way of knowing so different from the others.

Perhaps the most important feature of science is that it demands a willingness to judge situations based on the quality of evidence rather than on one's preconceptions (which include personal experiences, beliefs, biases). This doesn't mean that a scientist's preconceptions are unimportant; in fact, they often work to shape one's questions, one's ideas, and even one's theories. The crucial point, however, is that questions, ideas, and theories are not evidence, and a scientist must ultimately be willing to modify his or her preconceptions – or even admit that they were wrong – if quality evidence repeatedly fails to confirm them. For several years, thousands of doctors and female patients *knew,* for example, that hormone-replacement therapy was an effective way of dealing with the hormonal changes brought on by menopause. Only it wasn't. Scientific research at the National Institutes of Health proved that being on hormone-replacement therapy actually *increased* a woman's chances of suffering heart failure, and as a result, thousands of women wisely stopped the treatment.

If we're going to privilege scientific evidence, we have to draw some boundary conditions around what science *can* and *cannot* do. Not every question can be answered scientifically. For instance, religious beliefs, personal ethics, and notions of morality are among the types of ideas that no one needs to change if they don't match up with scientific evidence, because these types of ideas are not **empirical**. That is, beliefs, ethics, and morals are not ideas about *physical reality,* but about our spirituality and personal convictions. As such, these are entirely removed from the realm in which science operates and are not, therefore, subject to any of the requirements of the scientific process. Questions about the physical universe, however, are answered for scientists through the collection and analysis of scientific evidence.

So what makes knowledge *scientific?* First, the knowledge has to be **verifiable**, which means that you have to be able to prove the idea to be true. This immediately separates scientific knowledge from most forms of religious knowledge; whereas religious truths are accepted by faith, scientific truths are accepted only if they can be verified with appropriate tests. Take the idea that men are more talkative than women. Is this verifiable? Could we construct a study that would test this idea? Yes – and it doesn't matter if you aren't exactly sure how such a test would be done. In other words, asking if an idea is verifiable isn't the same as asking whether *you would know how* to verify it. Instead, the idea just has to be verifiable in principle. For example, Einstein proposed that light is bent by gravity – this is verifiable in principle, even though it was many more years before the technology existed to actually test it.

Along with being verifiable, scientific knowledge has to be **falsifiable** – that is, you have to be able to prove it wrong. At first glace, it might seem that if a prediction can be proven true then it can also be proven false, but that's not necessarily the case. Consider this prediction: *Every person either does or does not love chocolate.* Is this verifiable? Yes – we could design a test to prove this prediction true. However, it is not falsifiable, because there is absolutely no situation (whether real or imagined) that would prove it false. The reason is that every possibility is contained in the prediction. Everyone is either *X* or *not X*. As a result, any study that tested this prediction would confirm it, no matter what the data showed. (What about people who just *like* chocolate? Aren't they exceptions to the prediction? No: if they *love* it, they're in the first group, and if they *don't love* it, they're in the second group. There are no other options.)

Verifiability and falsifiability are properties of ideas. In order to be considered scientific knowledge, an idea must also have **empirical support**, which means that it actually *has* been tested and showed to be true. What about the thousand people who prayed for their relatives, and the relatives recovered – isn't that enough proof? No; testing an idea through personal experience isn't enough, because there's too great a risk that other things might have caused the outcome besides what you're actually looking at. A thousand prayers and a thousand recoveries sounds impressive, yes, but let's not forget that most medical problems resolve themselves. Would the patients have recovered anyway, even without the prayers? We don't know. How about people who have been prayed for and yet have not recovered? Are they just exceptions to the rule, or are we seeing something that isn't really there? Did all of the thousand recovering patients know they were being prayed for? Did they all believe prayer would heal them? Do these things matter?

These are just a few of the unanswered questions that knowledge from personal experience leaves us with. But these are important questions. Let's say doctors are designing a new drug to combat obesity. To test it, they give the drug to a thousand overweight people, and all of those people lose weight while they're on the drug. Would that be enough proof that the drug works? Just like with the prayer example, it would seem to be, but it isn't. Maybe those people would have lost weight anyway. The only way to rule out this alternative explanation is to compare our results with those of overweight people who *didn't* take the drug. This latter group of people is called a **control group**. If people in the control group lose weight to the same degree as those taking our drug, then we can be reasonably sure that the drug doesn't work.

Maybe it wasn't the drug itself that caused the weight loss, but the participants' belief in the drug. If they thought the drug was going to help them lose weight, maybe that belief was enough to explain their weight loss. The only way to rule out this alternative explanation is to make everyone on our **experimental group** (those taking the drug) believe they're taking the drug, but actually to give some people a **placebo** instead. A placebo is something that looks, feels, and tastes exactly like the drug being tested, but is, in fact, something like a sugar pill that has no actual active ingredient. Now, if everybody in the experiment (those taking the real drug plus those taking the placebo) loses weight to the same degree, then we can be fairly certain that the drug had little to do with it.

What we're describing here is known in scientific research as a **double-blind, placebo-controlled (DBPC) experiment**. It is double-blind if neither the patients in the experimental group, nor the doctors who actually give them the drugs, know whether an individual patient is receiving the real drug or the placebo. This is important because either the doctors or the patients (or both) might behave differently if they knew which condition the patient was in. The purpose of such an experiment, as you might have gathered, is to rule out **rival explanations** – that is, other ways of explaining why a particular event occurred. Only by doing this can we have much confidence in the accuracy of what we're seeing.

One could do the same thing in the prayer example. One rival explanation for the finding that prayed-for people recovered is that they would have recovered anyway. Another is that it was the patients' own beliefs in the power of prayer, rather than the prayers themselves, that mattered. How could we rule out these explanations scientifically? We could rule out the first one by using a control group: a group of people with medical problems similar to those in our experimental group who are *not* prayed for. If prayer aids in healing, then the experimental group should recover faster, or more often, or more fully than the control group. If they don't, then we can't conclude that the prayers were helpful. We could rule out the second rival explanation by making sure that our experimental group consisted of some people who believed in the power of prayer and some who did not. If it is the prayers themselves that matter, then both of these groups should heal at the same rate.

This is just a short introduction to what it means to study something scientifically. Scientists use their intuition, personal experience, and even their knowledge by authority just like anyone else does – but, for questions having to do with physical reality (which includes human behavior), they subordinate those forms of knowledge to scientific knowledge. Sometimes that means they have to admit that their intuition or experience was actually wrong. Scientists don't get to cling to their ideas if the evidence repeatedly fails to support them. To be fair, most of us don't do that even with our own personal experience – if we try something several times and it never works, most of us give up on it. The difference between this and scientific testing is a matter of how much confidence we can have in the "evidence" we collect.

This information we present in this book is scientific. It is not based on our personal ideas, experiences, intuitions, or beliefs. Now, that doesn't mean that all of it is 100% correct. Science can still make mistakes, just like any other way of knowing can. However, those who understand the scientific method can have a greater degree of confidence in the accuracy of the information than if it *were* simply a reflection of our experiences or beliefs. Science works harder than any other way of knowing to test and scrutinize the accuracy of its information – so even though science is sometimes wrong, it's a better bet for your money.

As an aside, there actually is scientific evidence that prayer can be effective in healing. In a randomized double-blind study, Sicher, Targ, Moore, and Smith (1998) recruited distant healers to pray for 20 adult patient with advanced AIDS, while another 20 patients (matched with the experimental group by age, $CD4^+$ count, and number of AIDS-defining diseases) did not receive the extra prayer. Both the patients and their health care providers were unaware of which condition each patient was in (i.e., the experiment was double blind). After six months of the prayer intervention, those in the experimental group had acquired significantly fewer AIDS-defining illnesses, had lower illness severity, required significantly fewer doctor visits, fewer hospitalizations, and fewer days of hospitalization, and showed significantly improved mood, as compared to those in the control condition. Obviously, this is only one study, and science demands that findings be replicated before being generally accepted. The point, however, is that, for scientists, the question of whether prayer aids in healing (or any empirical question, for that matter) requires more than simple belief or anecdotal evidence; it requires rigorous scientific investigation.

We've now introduced you to the idea of studying biological influences on communication behavior and given you a primer on the scientific method. To close this chapter, let us preview what awaits you in the rest of this book.

A Preview of this Book

The remaining chapters in this book are of two types. Chapters Two through Five will introduce you to several of the major bodily systems we'll be discussing. These include the brain, the nervous system, the endocrine system, and the muscular system. These chapters are designed to give you a basic introduction to the anatomy of the system being described. Each chapter will begin with an overview of the structure and function of the system. It will then discuss methods used to study the effects of that system on human communication, and finally, it will address some applications of that research to our understanding of communication behavior.

By contrast, Chapters Six through Eleven address various communication contexts and behaviors, such as conflict, love, stress, emotion, attraction, and parenting. Unlike in the first half, each chapter in the second half of the book consists of narrative descriptions of scientific studies on the connection between communication and biology. These descriptions are designed to give you an understanding of what research in each of these context areas has discovered about the biology-communication connection, without requiring you to be an expert in the methods or measurements.

As you read the chapters in this book, bear in mind that we wrote them assuming very little knowledge on our readers' part about anatomy, physiology, research methods, or statistics. Our descriptions are therefore intentionally simple, and we invite you to read more in the areas that interest you. Almost all of the research we review in this book has been conducted outside the field of communication, and so many communication students might never be exposed to it otherwise. Our goal, therefore, is to bring this knowledge to you, in the hopes that it will help you to appreciate the magnificent and awe-inspiring ways that our minds and bodies work together to help us communicate with one another.

Key Terms

Control group
Deterministic fallacy
Double-blind, placebo-controlled (DBPC) experiment
Empirical
Empirical support
Epistemology
Experimental group
Falsifiable
Immutability fallacy
Naturalistic fallacy
Placebo
Rival explanations
Verifiable

Chapter Two: The Brain

Brain is an Old English word for the three-pound mass of tissue and nerves enclosed in your skull. At first glance, it may not look like much: just a wrinkled mound of pinkish gray tissue with the texture of cold oatmeal. Its unimpressive appearance belies its remarkable abilities, however. Along with the nervous system (which we discuss in the next chapter), the brain controls pretty much everything you do every moment of your life, and so it is well worth our attention.

We begin this chapter by discussing the structure and function of the brain. You will learn that the brain can be divided into four major structures and serves a number of important functions with respect to communication. Next, we'll discuss some of the many methods that scientists have developed for measuring neurological activity. Finally, we will address some important applications of neurology to the understanding of human communication.

Structure and Function of the Brain

The brain is a needy organ. It accounts for only about 2% of your body weight, yet it demands 20% of your body's fuel. About a fifth of the blood your heart pumps is sent to the brain. The brain has no moving parts and is about 80% water. It has four major regions, which we will discuss separately in this section. These are the **cerebrum**, the **diencephalon**, the **brain stem**, and the **cerebellum**.

The Cerebrum

When you think about the appearance of the brain, you probably picture the cerebrum. The cerebrum is the largest part of the brain, accounting for about 85% of its total weight. It is gray and wrinkly and looks much like a large walnut. The cerebrum is made up of **gray matter** and **white matter**, each of which consists of different types of nerve fibers that control different cognitive and motor functions.

The ridges that cover the outer surface of the cerebrum are called **gyri**, and the shallow grooves that separate them are called **sulci**. The cerebrum also has a smaller number of deeper grooves, which are called **fissures**. One, in particular – the *longitudinal fissure* – runs down the center of the cerebrum and divides it into two **cerebral hemispheres**, the left and the right. The hemispheres are connected by a set of fibers known as the **corpus callosum**, which acts to transmit information between the left and right sides of the cerebrum. We will discuss the differences between the cerebral hemispheres later in this chapter.

The cerebrum is further divided into different sections, called lobes. The largest is the **frontal lobe**, which is located in the front and top of the cerebrum. Behind it is the **parietal lobe**, and at the back of the cerebrum is the **occipital lobe**. On each side of the cerebrum, right above the ears, are the **temporal lobes**. Each lobe is named for the bones of the skull that lie over them, and each lobe houses different control areas that oversee specific functions in the body.

The frontal and temporal lobes house two important control areas for communication. The first is **Broca's area**, which is named for French surgeon Pierre Paul Broca who first described it in 1861. Broca's area is located (in most people) in the frontal lobe of the left hemisphere, just in front of the left temporal lobe. It is the area of the brain that controls your ability to speak. It affects how you understand language and it controls the movement of the tongue, lips, and vocal cords when you produce speech. When people have damage to this part of the brain, which is known as **Broca's aphasia**, they are unable to make grammatically correct sentences. They often know what they want to say, but are not able to vocalize the words.

One of the most important parts of the temporal lobes is **Wernicke's area**, first described in the late 19th Century by a German anatomist named Carl Wernicke. In most people, Wernicke's area is located on the upper portion of the left temporal lobe. It plays a critical role in our ability to interpret spoken and written language. When we hear or read a sentence, Wernicke's area helps us to understand the meaning and significance of the words, and Broca's area helps us to understand the syntax and determine whether the sentence is grammatically correct. Damage to this area of the brain, which is known as **Wernicke's aphasia**, causes people to lose their ability to create meaningful sentences or expressions. Their words have correct grammatical structure but they don't have any meaning.

The Diencephalon

The diencephalon is located at the top of the brain stem and is enclosed entirely by the cerebrum. For that reason, it is sometimes also called the *interbrain.* There are three major structures in the diencephalon: the **thalamus**, the **hypothalamus**, and the **epithalamus**. The thalamus is an egg-shaped mass of gray tissue that sits between the two cerebral hemispheres. Its job is to relay sensory information to the cerebrum. Information from all of our senses – except for our sense of smell – passes through the nerves to the thalamus and is then relayed to the cerebrum. The cerebrum interprets that information and then sends instructions back to the thalamus for muscle movement.

The hypothalamus (which literally means *under the thalamus*) is about the size of two peas and weighs about a fifth of an ounce. It is located on the lowermost part of the diencephalon and is responsible for controlling a number of bodily functions, including temperature, digestion, water balance, the production of gastric acid, breathing, and sleep. More important for communication scholars, the hypothalamus is a component of the **limbic system**, which is a collection of organs that play a large role in the management of emotion. Hunger, thirst, pain, pleasure, and sex drive all emanate from the hypothalamus. It is also responsive to stress, releasing particular hormones that help prepare the body to handle stressful situations. We will discuss these hormones and their function in greater detail in Chapter Four.

The epithalamus is the third important structure in the diencephalon. It houses the pineal gland (which is part of the endocrine system, discussed in Chapter Four), and the choroids plexus, which forms cerebrospinal fluid.

The Brain Stem

The brain stem is about three inches long and is about as wide in diameter as your thumb. It is the most ancient part of the brain; in fact, the human brain stem is not substantially different in structure or function than the brains of many reptiles. For this reason, the brain stem is sometimes referred to as the **reptilian brain**.

Three structures make up the brain stem: the **midbrain**, the **pons**, and the **medulla oblongata**. The midbrain is about two and a half centimeters long and is located between the cerebrum and the pons. It is comprised of nuclei that control reflex actions, such as blinking, pupil dilation, and focusing in the eye, as well as the adjustment of the ears to sound volume. Nuclei in the midbrain also control movements of the neck and head in response to things we see or hear. For example, when you see something traveling swiftly toward your face, your natural reflex is to pull your head backward – the nuclei in the midbrain help make this happen.

The pons (which is Latin for *bridge*) is a bundle of white matter that is about an inch wide. As its name suggests, it serves as a connection or bridge between the two halves of the cerebellum. It also connects each half of the cerebellum with the opposite half of the cerebrum. At the very bottom of the brain stem is the medulla oblongata. It contains nuclei that control functions such as heart rate, breathing, blood pressure, and swallowing. It is also the part of the brain that makes you vomit! The medulla oblongata connects directly to the spinal cord.

All along the brain stem is a mass of gray matter known as the **reticular formation**. Its function is to monitor incoming signals to determine which ones can be safely ignored and which ones need to be passed on to the brain. For instance, stop reading for a moment and think about how many different things you can hear right now. Depending on where you are, you might hear footsteps, people talking, a radio or television, the air conditioner, the tick of a clock, and the rustle of your clothing as you move. Now, think about how many different things you can see right now. In addition to this book, you see your own body, the chair you're sitting in, the walls around you, and dozens of other things in your immediate environment. Imagine if you had to pay attention to everything you heard or saw all the time. The sheer volume of sensory information you take in at any given moment is overwhelming – and if you had to attend to every piece of information, it would quickly incapacitate you. The reticular formation gives you the ability to concentrate on the information that matters, while ignoring most of the other sensory information you are taking in each second.

The Cerebellum

At the bottom of the brain, underneath the cerebrum and just behind the brain stem, is the cerebellum, which literally means *little brain.* The cerebellum looks a little like a piece of cauliflower. Its three primary jobs are to coordinate muscle movement, regulate muscle tone, and help us to maintain equilibrium, or balance. It is responsible for your ability to stand up, walk, hit a baseball, touch your finger to your nose, or do any number of relatively automated movements. When people suffer damage to the cerebellum, they often have trouble with balance, suffer from tremors, or become clumsy and uncoordinated.

The cerebellum does not engage in any conscious activity. Rather, it works automatically by receiving information directly from a number of muscular and sensory organs. Such information helps the cerebellum to monitor and modify muscle movements. The cerebellum also receives information from the cerebrum and issues appropriate instructions to the muscular system. As a result, the cerebellum is sometimes referred to as the brain's "autopilot."

We have now covered the basic anatomy of the brain. Since the brain controls most of what we do at any given moment, it is easy to see why researchers who investigate communication behavior would be interested in studying the brain. There's one small problem, however: the brain is well protected by thick skull bones and several layers of buffering material. It's not as if we can take people's brains out, study them, and then give them back. So how do social scientists study brain activity? We describe some of the various ways in the next section.

Measuring Brain Activity

Over the years, researchers have developed a number of different ways to measure the brain's activities. Some of these methods are designed to make use of the brain's electrical activity, whereas others make use of differences in the physical and chemical properties of the brain. In this section, we will briefly introduce you to four methods of measuring neurological activity.

The Electroencephalogram

The **electroencephalogram** (or **EEG**) is a technique that records the electrical activity of large regions of the brain. Application of the use of EEG on human brains was developed in the early 1930s, although researchers had known that the brain produces electrical waves since the late 1800s. In a typical EEG experiment, electrodes are attached to a participant's scalp in a specific pattern that corresponds to particular areas of the brain. The electrodes are connected to magnets, which are connected (in the traditional form of the test) to pens that map the participant's "brain waves" onto a moving sheet of paper (much like the graphing of seismic activity during an earthquake).

The brain waves that the EEG records are representations of the brain's electrical activity, and surgical research has shown that they are similar when measured from the surface of the scalp and when measured directly from the brain tissue (although they are stronger when measured directly from the brain). There are several different types of brain waves; they differ from each other in their frequency and amplitude, and also in the situations in which they are observed. *Alpha waves* are produced when a person sits quietly, in a relaxed position, with his or her eyes closed. They have high amplitude (meaning that the waves are tall when graphed) and moderate frequency (meaning that there is moderate distance between each wave when graphed). Typically, alpha waves will disappear when the person begins a specific cognitive activity (e.g., figuring out a math problem) and/or opens his or her eyes. *Beta waves* are produced during periods of excitement, arousal, or pronounced mental or physical activity. Compared to alpha waves, beta waves have lower amplitude and higher frequency. *Delta waves* are high amplitude, low frequency waves that appear (in normal humans) only during deep sleep. When delta waves are observed in someone who is awake, they can be indications of some type of brain abnormality, such as a tumor. Other types of waves include *theta, kappa, lambda, mu,* and *gamma waves.*

Positron-Emission Tomography

Another method for assessing neurological activity is **positron-emission tomography** (or **PET**). Unlike EEG, PET makes use of the brain's chemical activities. In a PET, either a small amount of radioactively labeled water is injected into a person's bloodstream or the person inhales a gas containing a radioactive molecule. These are not harmful to a patient because the radioactive molecules break down within just a few minutes. In the process of doing so, however, they release particles called positrons, which collide with electrons in the brain. These collisions produce photons, which can be detected by a PET scanner as they exit the head. A computer then reconstructs changes in the density of the flow of particles from different areas of the brain, and an image of activity in particular brain regions is produced.

PET can be used, therefore, to investigate which parts of the brain are activated when people see, hear, or think about particular things. For example, a researcher might be interested in finding out which areas of the brain are activated when people look at pictures of their loved ones. In such a study, participants' brains would be scanned while they look at the stimulus pictures, and the images produced could then be compared with the brain scans of people looking at pictures of strangers. This type of comparison would help the researcher to determine the location(s) of neurological activity that people experience when they see pictures of people they love.

Magnetic Resonance Imaging

In some ways, **magnetic resonance imaging** (or **MRI**) is similar to PET. Both use a large tubular machine that patients enter while lying down, and both produce images of the brain itself, rather than brain waves (as in EEG). Unlike PET, however, MRI makes use of the movements of hydrogen protons rather than the breaking down of radioactive molecules. Here's how an MRI works. The nucleus of a hydrogen atom (which consists of a single proton) acts like a spinning bar magnet; as each proton spins, one end acts like a north pole and the other end acts like a south pole of a bar magnet. Under normal circumstances, the protons of hydrogen atoms are positioned randomly, meaning that they spin in any number of directions. When a person enters an MRI machine, however, a magnetic field causes all of the protons to become aligned (just like the needle of a compass is aligned with the Earth's magnetic field).

To understand how the MRI produces an image of the brain, it is important to know two things: protons generate an electrical current when they spin, and proton density varies in different types of brain tissues. When the protons are all aligned (as they are in the MRI's magnetic field), the MRI uses the electrical current they generate to produce proton-density images of the brain. An MRI produces images that represent "slices" of the brain (as if you held a knife horizontally against your forehead and sliced through to the back of your head). A computer can also be used to produce two- or three-dimensional images of the brain.

Functional Magnetic Resonance Imaging

A technique known as **functional magnetic resonance imaging** (or **fMRI**) is not really a different procedure than MRI, but it works on a different principle. As neurons in the brain become activated, they consume more oxygen than normal. This causes a temporary dip in the oxygen content of the blood, so the blood vessels compensate by expanding so that more blood can flow to those neurons. This increase in blood flow actually brings more blood (and thus, more oxygen) to the neurons than they can use, resulting in an increase in the overall amount of oxygen in that region of the brain. When the oxygen content of blood changes, the blood's magnetic properties also change, and MRI can detect and identify these changes in particular areas of the brain. The images produced are called fMRIs.

Electroencephalogram, positron-emission tomography, magnetic resonance imaging, and functional magnetic resonance imaging are not the only procedures available for studying brain activity, but they are among the most commonly used. Each has its advantages and disadvantages. PET, MRI, and fMRI all require very expensive equipment and extensively trained personnel to conduct; EEG is comparatively much easier and less expensive. However, EEG produces only graphs of brain wave activity, whereas the other procedures produce actual brain images. Researchers must weigh these and other pros and cons when designing their studies.

Because of the cost and expertise required, these procedures have seldom been used by scholars attempting to understand human communication. By contrast, other, less sophisticated, approaches have characterized communication research. Nonetheless, these applications have raised important and interesting questions, and have provided a glimpse into the many ways that the brain affects, and is affected by, communicative processes. We discuss some of these applications in the following section.

Applications to Human Communication

Few communication researchers have been actively engaged in studying the brain. Notable exceptions include research on temperament and on hemispheric dominance. We will discuss each of these applications in this section.

Temperament

The simplest way to think about your **temperament** is as a snapshot of your personality. We all know people who are high-strung, naïve, shy, obsessive, or maybe just plain nuts. When we describe someone's temperament, we're describing the way that person is under most circumstances. Of course, shy people are outgoing and high-strung people are quiet once in a while, but we still describe them as shy or high-strung because that's how they usually are.

What makes up a personality? Research on the dimensions of personality has had a long history and researchers have answered this question in a number of different ways. Today, one of the most commonly used ways of thinking about personality is as a combination of three "super traits": **psychoticism**, **extraversion**, and **neuroticism** (Eysenck & Eysenck, 1985). Psychoticism might sound scary, but it's just a measure of your impulsiveness or self-control. When someone makes you angry, for instance, do you usually keep your cool and let it pass, or do you like to get back at them? This is one example of a difference between someone who would score low (keep your cool) or high (get them back) on psychoticism. Extraversion has to do with how outgoing you are and how much external stimulation you like. Maybe you're someone who loves meeting new people, always likes to be around activity, and gets bored with spending quiet time alone. If so, you'd probably score high on a measure of extraversion. By contrast, people who are more introverted like solitude more and prefer the company of smaller groups of people they already know to larger groups of people they haven't met. Finally, neuroticism has to do with how much anxiety you typically feel. If people describe you as a "worrier," you're probably high in neuroticism; if you're more carefree or "happy-go-lucky," your level of neuroticism is likely to be low.

In the communication field, researchers have looked at the relationship between temperament and communication from a perspective known as **communibiology**. The basic premise of communibiology is simple: all human activity – whether kinesic, cognitive, or emotional – depends on the brain. Because humans are living organisms, neither their thoughts and feelings, nor their behavior, can be separate from the activity of their bodies; therefore, all thoughts, feelings, and behavior are, in a very real sense, biologically based. That doesn't mean that our biology *determines* our behavior (in the sense that we can't control what we do). Rather, it suggests that we are predisposed by our brains to behave in certain ways at certain times.

What does communibiology have to do with temperament? Beatty and McCroskey and their colleagues (Beatty & McCroskey, 1997,

1998, 2000a, b; Beatty, McCroskey, & Heisel, 1998; Beatty, McCroskey, & Valencic, 2001) have proposed that the three fundamental components of personality – psychoticism, extraversion, and neuroticism – are controlled in various ways by three neurological emotion systems described by Gray (1991). The first is the **behavioral inhibition system**. This is responsible for the immediate halting of behavior in the face of threat (or the "deer in the headlights" phenomenon), and it is thought to involve a number of areas of the brain, including the hypothalamus, the amygdala, and the basal nuclei. The second emotion system is the **behavioral approach system**, which is best thought of as the system that motivates you to engage in behaviors that are rewarding. For example, when you see an attractive person at a party, your behavioral approach system kicks into gear, giving you the drive to strike up a conversation with him or her. This system is thought to involve basal nuclei and fibers from the midbrain. Finally, you have probably already heard of the **fight or flight system**. It gives you a burst of energy when you perceive a threat, either so you can fight that threat or flee from it. It is thought to involve several parts of the brain, including the amygdala, the hypothalamus, and the nuclei of the brain stem.

Communibiologists such as Beatty and McCroskey have argued that measuring a person's personality traits (i.e., his or her levels of psychoticism, extraversion, and neuroticism) provides a type of snapshot of his or her underlying neurological processes in these three emotion systems. In a series of studies, Beatty and McCroskey and their colleagues have shown that various temperament traits (which they connect to the brain's emotion systems) influence how people behave in communicative contexts. Here's one example that you can probably relate to. As you know, many people have a fear of public speaking – in fact, people consistently say they fear public speaking even more than they fear death! Perhaps you've had to give presentations in your classes and have experienced a high degree of anxiety, so you know what we're talking about.

Beatty and Valencic (2000) designed a study to determine two things: first, whether an aspect of temperament known as **communication apprehension** makes a difference in how nervous people are before giving a speech, and second, whether it makes any difference if the speech requires a lot of preparation or not very much at all. Communication apprehension can be defined as the level of anxiety a person feels over having to communicate with others (as in a public speaking situation), and communibiologists have suggested that is directly related to the interplay between one's behavioral inhibition and behavioral approach systems. So, it makes sense to expect that your level of communication apprehension would affect how nervous you are before giving a speech. Should it matter how much preparation the speech requires, though? You've probably had to put together presentations that require outlines, handouts, visual aids, and a great deal of preparation – and you've probably also had to give short, informal presentations that don't require any advance planning at all. Does either type of speech make you more nervous than the other?

In their study of 63 college students, Beatty and Valencic found that communication apprehension made a big difference in how nervous people were before having to give a speech. (Recall that communication apprehension is defined as a temperament trait, so it should not change much from day to day within each person.) However, they also found that the preparation required for the speech made *no difference* in how nervous participants were. Only their communication apprehension mattered.

It might be tempting to conclude from this study that communibiologists think the brain is the only thing that matters in how we communicate. That's not the case, however. Researchers working to understand communication from a biological perspective agree that biology is only one influence out of many that make a difference in how people communicate with each other.

Hemispheric Dominance

We have already explained that the cerebrum is divided into two halves, or hemispheres. You might already know that each hemisphere controls the body's opposite side – for instance, the left hemisphere controls the right arm and the right hemisphere the left. What you might not know is that each hemisphere specializes in specific types of tasks. In most people, for instance, the left hemisphere is dominant for language and the right hemisphere is dominant for nonverbal communication (such as interpreting gestures or facial expressions). That does not mean that only the left hemisphere is involved in language or that only the right hemisphere is involved in nonverbal behavior. Instead, the two hemispheres function interdependently, with each taking the lead on certain types of tasks.

We said above that this was the pattern of hemispheric dominance in most people. For that reason, we say that these people have **standard dominance**. A large majority of the population – and an even larger majority of right-handed people – have standard dominance (SD). These people have strong left hemisphere specialization for language and verbal communication and strong right hemisphere specialization for nonverbal communication. In addition, the left hemisphere in SD people is responsible for logical, analytical, and social interpretations of incoming information, whereas the right hemisphere is responsible for analogic, emotive, and holistic interpretation of the same information. For instance, people with standard dominance process logical issues primarily in the left hemisphere but process emotion primarily in the right.

There are two other options, though. About a third of the population has what is referred to as **anomalous dominance** (AD). The AD brain is characterized by one of two processing patterns. The usual specializations of the left and right hemispheres might be reversed, compared to the SD brain; in that case, the right hemisphere specializes in language and logic, and the left specializes in nonverbal communication and emotion. It can also be the case that, compared to SD brains, AD brains are simply more symmetrical, such that neither hemisphere truly dominates. You are more likely to have anomalous dominance if you or your family members are left-handed.

Finally, some people don't really fit into either the SD or AD categories, and so we say that such people have **mixed dominance** (MD). The MD brain has markers of *both* standard *and* anomalous dominance. Consequently, MD individuals may have left hemisphere specialization in some types of verbal and nonverbal tasks and right hemisphere specialization in others. Having mixed dominance is a little like being ambidextrous (being able to write with either hand). It might surprise you to know that mixed dominance is probably the least studied of the three dominance patterns. This is because researchers may choose to compare only SD and AD individuals in their studies, to maximize the differences between groups.

What does research on hemispheric dominance have to tell us about human communication? In this section, we'll review some findings with respect to communicator style, emotion, and relational behavior. You should not take this to be an exhaustive review of the literature on hemispheric dominance – it is far from it. However, this will give you an idea of some of the things research has discovered about the links between hemispheric dominance and communicative behavior.

You might think of *communicator style* as your "communication temperament." It's a way of describing how you typically communicate with other people: for instance, are you friendly? Reserved? Dramatic? Contentious? You can probably think of someone you would describe in one or more of these ways. And, as with your personality, your communicator style isn't set in stone: even if you are a very friendly person, that doesn't mean you're going to be friendly in *every* situation, just in *most* situations.

Bodary and Miller (2000) conducted a study to see whether people's communicator styles were related to their hemispheric dominance. Most people don't already know what their own hemispheric dominance is, so to find out, Bodary and Miller had participants in their study complete three different self-report measures. We noted above that people with SD brains are likely to be right-handed and that people with AD brains are likely to be left-handed. Thus, the first measure Bodary and Miller used was a measure of **sinistrality**, or handedness. The second measure also assessed sinistrality, but for participants' *family members* rather than for the participants themselves. Finally, the researchers gave participants a list of immune disorders and learning disorders and asked them to indicate how many of the disorders, if any, they had experienced. This measure was used because people with SD brains are less likely than those with AD or MD brains to suffer from immune or learning disorders, so this is another marker of hemispheric dominance.

Bodary and Miller ended up with 592 people in their study. Only about a quarter of the participants (24.7%) were classified as SD on the basis of their sinistrality and disorder scores. Most (62.3%) were classified as MD, and the rest (13.0%) were classified as AD. The researchers excluded all MD participants from the rest of the study, in order to look just at the difference between SD and AD individuals. They gave the remaining participants a self-report measure of communicator style, which assesses ten distinct components of an individual's "style" of communicating: dominant, dramatic, contentious, animated, memorable (or impression-leaving), precise, relaxed, attentive, open, and friendly. The measure also includes an eleventh component, communicator image, which is an overall assessment of one's communicator style.

When they compared SD and AD participants, Bodary and Miller found that the two groups differed significantly on three of the components of communicator style. Specifically, AD participants reported that they were more animated, more dramatic, and more open than SD participants. This finding suggests that hemispheric dominance has only a few effects on how people see their own communication styles. Does hemispheric dominance affect their actual communication skills, however? A study by Floyd and Mikkelson (2003) looked at whether hemispheric dominance influences people's abilities to decode facial displays of emotion accurately. Floyd and Mikkelson used the same measures of hemispheric dominance that were used by Bodary and Miller. After having 531 participants complete the measures, Floyd and Mikkelson classified 70.4% of their sample as SD, 18.8% as MD, and the rest (10.8%) as AD. They then had participants do an exercise in which they were shown a series of ten photographs of the same face making ten different emotional expressions (e.g., smiling, frowning, looking scared). They were also given a list of ten emotions (e.g., happy, angry, disgusted) and were asked to match each emotion with the picture of the face displaying that emotion.

It may seem like an easy task, but the average score of the participants (out of 10 possible correct answers) was only 6.5. Did the average score differ among SD, MD, and AD people? Not on its own. However, when Floyd and Mikkelson further divided each hemispheric dominance group into men and women, they found that the six groups (SD men, SD women, MD men, MD women, AD men, AD women) differed significantly from each other in how accurate they were at decoding the emotion displays. Women with MD brains did the best – an average of 7 out of 10 correct answers. By contrast, men with MD brains did the worst – an average of only 5.9 correct answers. The SD and AD participants were in between, which may strike you as odd, given that you might expect those with *mixed* dominance to be in the middle. When it comes to decoding facial expressions of emotion, however, it appears that having an MD brain is an advantage for women but a disadvantage for men.

To be certain, research on temperament and hemispheric dominance are not the only potential applications of neurology to the study of human communication. In fact, researchers in other social scientific fields have used brain-imaging techniques to study topics highly relevant to human communication, such as emotion or attraction. As communication scientists become more familiar with the methods and applications of brain-imaging tools, the opportunities to study communicative phenomena will greatly expand.

Key Terms

Anomalous dominance
Behavioral approach system
Behavioral inhibition system
Brain stem
Broca's aphasia
Broca's area
Cerebellum
Cerebral hemisphere
Cerebrum
Communibiology
Communication apprehension
Corpus callosum
Diencephalon
EEG
Electroencephalogram
Epithalamus
Extraversion
Fight or flight system
Fissures
fMRI
Frontal lobe
Functional magnetic resonance imaging
Gray matter
Gyri
Hypothalamus
Limbic system
Magnetic resonance imaging
Medulla oblongata
Midbrain
Mixed dominance
MRI
Neuroticism
Occipital lobe
Parietal lobe
PET
Pons
Positron-emission tomography
Psychoticism
Reptilian brain
Reticular formation
Sinistrality

Standard dominance
Sulci
Temperament
Temporal lobe
Thalamus
Wernicke's aphasia
Wernicke's area
White matter

Chapter Three: The Nervous System

Along with the brain, the nervous system is truly "master and commander" of the body. It governs every thought you think, every feeling you feel, and every action you undertake. Getting dressed, driving a car, preparing a meal, petting a dog, and even reading this book are just a few examples of the thousands of things your nervous system allows you to do each day. Consequently, it also affects people's communication behaviors in a variety of ways.

In this chapter, we will discuss the structure and function of the nervous system, paying particular attention to the autonomic division. We will then describe some of the "markers" of nervous system activity that researchers measure. Finally, we will introduce you to some of the studies that have examined nervous system activity in the context of human communication, and comment on other applications that await attention.

Structure and Function of the Nervous System

When we refer to the body's nervous system, we are actually talking about several different systems that work together to keep the body running efficiently. In this section, we will describe the basic structure of the nervous system, the functions that each structure has, and the things that make the nervous system work. We begin by discussing the various structures that comprise the nervous system.

Mapping the Body's Nervous System

The nervous system is actually a combination of two separate but related systems: the **central nervous system** and the **peripheral nervous system**. The central nervous system consists of the brain and the spinal cord and is really the "command center" of the entire body. As we mentioned in the previous chapter, the brain has primary responsibility for all physical and mental functions in the body. It is connected at its base to the spinal cord, which is a long structure consisting of nerves, gray matter, and white matter. The spinal cord has two primary functions. First, it relays information and instructions between the brain and the spinal nerves. The spinal nerves control most of the skeletal muscles in the body, as well as smooth muscles and glands. Second, the spinal cord controls many of our **reflexes**. For instance, if you accidentally touch something hot, you will pull your hand away immediately. It seems as though we do this automatically, without even thinking about it – and that's often literally true. When the spinal cord triggers a reflex, it often does so on its own, without waiting to consult the brain first. In this way, the spinal cord works to protect us from things in the environment that can be hazardous. When the spinal cord is damaged, as in a car crash, it often results in parts of the body being paralyzed.

Working with the central nervous system is the peripheral nervous system, which governs behavior and reactivity that are peripheral to the central nervous system's activities but are still essential for health and survival, such as digestion, blood flow, and **thermoregulation**, or the regulation of a consistent body temperature. The peripheral nervous system is comprised of two main parts: the **somatic nervous system** and the **autonomic nervous system**. The somatic nervous system controls the skeletal muscles, and so it is responsible for our ability to move our arms, legs, fingers, heads, or indeed any other parts of our bodies that have muscle attached. Consequently, the somatic nervous system is also responsible for our ability to make facial expressions, a topic we will take up in greater detail in Chapter Five.

The autonomic nervous system, which is the primary focus of this chapter, maintains regulatory functions in the body by controlling the body's internal organs. It is responsible, for instance, for keeping our hearts beating, our blood flowing, and our bodies operating efficiently.

The autonomic nervous system, or ANS, can be further divided into two units: the **sympathetic nervous system** and the **parasympathetic nervous system**. The sympathetic nervous system deals with the body's ability to become excited, energized, and aroused. When we exercise, for instance, it is the sympathetic nervous system that increases our heart rate and makes us sweat. When we get frightened, the sympathetic nervous system makes our pupils dilate and increases our blood pressure, giving us the burst of energy we need to either run or fight. By contrast, the parasympathetic nervous system deals with the body's ability to relax and rest. It is responsible for lowering heart rate and blood pressure after we are done exercising or after a threat or danger has passed. These two systems work together to increase our bodily energy when it is needed and to conserve it when it is not.

Various structures and chemicals help the various nervous systems do their jobs. In the next section, we briefly discuss two important chemical messengers used by the ANS, and the basic units of the nervous system that transmit its instructions to all parts of the body.

Helping the Nervous System Work

Catecholamines. The sympathetic nervous system generates arousal partly through release of two chemical messengers called **catecholamines**: **epinephrine** and **norepinephrine**. These function both as hormones and as **neurotransmitters**. Both epinephrine and norepinephrine are released into the bloodstream by the adrenal gland, which is part of the endocrine system, discussed in greater detail in Chapter Four. Epinephrine is better known as *adrenaline,* and it is responsible for the increased heart rate that we feel during periods of excitement or arousal. It produces what people sometimes refer to as an "adrenaline rush." When the sympathetic nervous system is activated, norepinephrine increases our blood pressure through vasoconstriction – that is, by constricting the blood vessels. These two catecholamines are released into the bloodstream fairly quickly following exposure to some type of stimulus, which might be the sound of a scream, the sight of an attractive person, or anything else that causes the body to become excited. Their job is to prepare the body for increased demands on its energy. For instance, when people experience stress, epinephrine and norepinephrine are secreted into the blood stream in order to provide their bodies with excess energy that they can use to deal with whatever is causing them stress.

Neurons. The basic unit of the nervous system is the **neuron**. Neurons are long, thin fibers found throughout the body that carry messages and instructions from the nervous system to muscles and organs through the use of electrical impulses. These impulses move along one neuron and then "jump" from one neuron to another at points of contact called **synapses**. As an illustration, imagine that you are sitting in your living room placing a telephone call to a friend. When you dial the telephone, it creates an electrical signal that travels from your living room to the telephone line outside your house. It then travels along the line in your neighborhood until it joins up with other lines that can carry it to the line in your friend's neighborhood. From there, it finds the line that goes into your friend's house and it makes his or her telephone ring. In a similar fashion, neurons carry electrical impulses from the nervous system to muscles or organs in order to make them respond to the instructions being given. Some neurons have synapses, or connections, with only one or two other neurons; some are connected with hundreds of others. Some neurons in the body can be up to three feet long.

There are three primary types of neurons. *Sensory neurons* are triggered by some type of physical stimulus in the environment, such as a light or a sound. Let's say that you're standing on the sidewalk and you suddenly hear what sounds like an explosion. The sensory neurons connected to your ears are immediately triggered. Importantly, the strength of the stimulus affects how strongly the sensory neuron responds – so, a very loud noise will produce a stronger reaction in your sensory neurons than a faint or quiet noise will.

When your sensory neurons are triggered, they activate *association neurons.* The association neurons take the information from your sensory neurons and translate it into commands for how your body should respond. For example, if you hear a loud "bang!" your sensory neurons will transmit that information to your association neurons, which will interpret the signals (e.g., "this sound is loud, is coming from a nearby source, and is probably associated with something that could be dangerous to the body") and then issue instructions for how to react (e.g., "the body should run away from the direction of the sound"). These commands are then transmitted to *motor neurons*, which make your body respond accordingly.

Interestingly, several drugs work by interfering with the way that neurons and synapses operate. For example, drugs that are stimulants (such as caffeine, cocaine, or amphetamines) reduce the strength of an outside stimulus that is needed to make sensory neurons fire. When people are on stimulants (e.g., when they have had several cups of coffee), their sensory neurons are triggered more frequently than normal, which produces a feeling of being more awake, alert, and energized. Drugs that are depressants (such as alcohol, marijuana, or heroin) do just the opposite – they make the neurons fire less frequently than they otherwise would.

In this section, we have described the fundamental structure of the nervous system and some of the features through which it does its work. How do communication researchers measure nervous system activity, however? In the next section, we describe some of the external activities that researchers measure in order to assess how the nervous system is reacting to various things. Our discussion will focus specifically on activities that are under the control of the autonomic nervous system.

Measuring Autonomic Nervous System Activity

When the ANS is activated, or aroused, it affects a number of different activities in the body that we will refer to here as physiological markers. These are things that researchers can measure and monitor to see how and when they change. In this section, we will discuss five physiological markers of ANS activation and describe the ways in which they are measured. These include heart rate, blood pressure, skin temperature, skin conductance, and pupil size. As we will discuss in the final section of this chapter, each of these markers has been studied in relation to various communicative and relational processes.

Heart Rate

The heart is an amazing muscle. It is only about the size of your fist, yet it works nonstop to keep blood circulating throughout the body. The average adult has about ten pints of blood in his or her body, and a healthy heart can pump that entire blood supply around the body about once every minute. What is most amazing about the heart is that it is one of a small number of muscles in the body that never gets tired out (the muscles that control the lungs and the movement of the eyes are other examples). In the span of 70 years, the heart will beat about *2.5 billion times* without ever needing to rest.

In healthy adults, the heart beats about 70 times per minute for men and about 80 times per minute for women when people are at rest (i.e., when they are not aroused or engaged in strenuous activity). However, heart rates fluctuate continually in response to a number of different stimuli, including how fast we breathe, how much activity we are engaged in, whether we are relaxed or excited, whether we are using any medications or drugs that alter the heart rate, and how warm or cold our environment is. Importantly, our heart rates also react to shifts in our emotion, a topic we will discuss in greater detail below.

In social science research, heart rate is typically measured in one of two ways: as beats per minute (**BPM**) or as an interbeat interval (**IBI**). BPM is based on the actual number of contractions the heart has during a 60-second period. Sometimes, researchers count the number of contractions within a shorter time frame (e.g., 15 seconds), and then multiply that number to arrive at a 60-second estimate. Larger values of BPM are associated with a faster heart rate.

IBI is based on the amount of time that lapses between heart contractions. As heart rate increases, IBI decreases. When your heart is beating very fast, the amount of time between each beat becomes very small. IBI can be estimated from BPM according to the following equation: IBI = 60,000/BPM.

Heart rate monitors that are available commercially usually use one of three devices for capturing the signal—a chest band, a wrist band, or an ear clip—each of which has its advantages and disadvantages. The chest band is often the most sensitive and accurate means of capturing the heart beat signal. It is also the most invasive because people must wear the band around their chests and against their skin. Wrist bands are less invasive but they can also be less accurate. The third device is a small clip that attaches to a person's ear lobe like a clip-on earring. This is probably the least invasive of the three means of capturing the signal, but it may have a tendency to restrict people's movement more than the other two.

Blood Pressure

Before we discuss blood pressure, let us briefly review how blood travels through the body. As you know, the heart controls the distribution of your blood supply. Each time it contracts, it pumps blood into your **arteries**, which carry that oxygen-rich blood to your brain and to other tissues in your body. The walls of your arteries have a wide middle layer of muscle fibers and elastic tissue that allows them to expand as blood rushes through them. After your brain and body tissues have "used" the blood brought to them by your arteries, that blood is carried back to the heart through your **veins**. Veins have thinner walls than arteries because the blood is under much lower pressure when it is being carried back to your heart than when your heart pumps it out. Blood veins also have special valves that prevent backflow. In addition to arteries and veins, you also have a number of **capillaries**, which are the smallest of all the blood vessels. Capillaries carry blood through your body tissues and they link the smallest branches of the arteries with the veins.

You probably already know that when you have your blood pressure taken, the result is a combination of two numbers: one number *over* another number. That's because blood pressure actually consists of two different types of pressure. **Systolic blood pressure** is an index of how much force is exerted against the walls of your arteries when your heart is contracting (i.e., during beats). This is the higher number in your blood pressure reading. By contrast, **diastolic blood pressure** is the level of force that is exerted against the walls of the arteries when the heart is resting (i.e., between beats). In fact, the terms *systole* and *diastole* mean *heart contraction* and *heart relaxation*, respectively.

Blood pressure is usually measured with a device called a **sphygmomanometer**, which consists of a cuff that wraps around your upper arm and a device for inflating it. When the cuff is inflated, it squeezes the arm to stop blood from flowing through the *brachial artery*, the blood vessel that supplies blood to the upper arm. A nurse or technician will slowly deflate the cuff and will listen, using a stethoscope, until a pulse can just barely be heard (this sound is referred to as a **Korotkoff sound**). The pressure of the cuff at this point indicates your systolic blood pressure. Then, the cuff is deflated even more until the pulse sound disappears. This indicates that the blood is again flowing freely along the artery. The pressure of the cuff at this point indicates your diastolic blood pressure.

Many people now use commercially available electronic sphygmomanometers to measure and monitor their own blood pressure at home. The device inflates automatically at the push of a button (instead of through the repeated squeezing of a bulb) and electronically records systolic and diastolic pressure. In research laboratories, blood pressure can also be measured using a method called **finger photoplethysmography**, in which a monitor attached to the fingertip uses the reflection of light from the skin surface and the red blood cells below to determine blood pressure.

Both systolic and diastolic blood pressure are measured in millimeters of mercury (mm Hg). For healthy adults, normal systolic blood pressure ranges from 95 to 140 mm Hg, with an average of 120. Normal diastolic blood pressure ranges from 60 to 89 mm Hg, with an average of 80. Thus, the average blood pressure for a healthy adult is 120 over 80. Resting blood pressure is higher in men than in women, however, from puberty through adulthood.

Skin Temperature

If you have ever put on a mood ring, you already know a little something about skin temperature. Skin temperature is an indirect measure of the amount of blood flow in skin tissue, and it is affected by emotion in a fairly direct way. When we experience emotional arousal (e.g., when we get angry or stressed), the surface temperature of our skin increases. This is because the sympathetic nervous system directs blood flow away from other parts of our bodies that are nonessential at the time (such as digestion) and toward the skin tissue as a way of preparing us for a fight-or-flight response. By contrast, when we experience arousal-inhibiting states such as fear, sadness, or depression, skin temperature decreases because the body does not have to be geared up for an immediate behavioral activation.

Shifts in blood flow to the skin tissue are sometimes directly observable. You probably know people who get red in the face when they get angry. This happens because more blood is flowing to the skin tissue and the surface temperature of the skin is increasing (perhaps this is why we refer to being angry as being "hot under the collar"). You may also have known people whose faces turn white when they get scared – hence the expression, "you look like you've just seen a ghost." This happens because fear induces the opposite effect: blood flow is directed away from the skin tissue, which causes the surface temperature of the skin to decrease (this may be why we refer to being fearful as "having cold feet"). Although they are by no means scientific instruments, mood rings operate on this same principle. Changes in skin temperature activate changes in the color of the ring, which are meant to indicate shifts in the mood of the wearer.

In fact, researchers who study emotion sometimes refer to emotions such as passion, anger, or jealousy as "hot emotions," and to emotions such as sadness, fear, or depression as "cold emotions," because of the kinds of effects these emotions have on our skin temperature. Skin temperature is usually measured with the use of **thermistor probes**, which attach to the surface of the skin and send temperature measurements to a computer that charts any changes in temperature over time.

Galvanic Skin Response

Galvanic skin response is an index of changes in electrical activity on the surface of the skin, or **skin conductance**, which are associated with how much perspiration is present on the skin surface. You probably already know that perspiration, or sweating, is the body's way to avoid overheating. Humans have between two and five million **eccrine sweat glands**, which are distributed over almost every part of the body surface. They are the most dense on the palms of the hands and the soles of the feet; in fact, one square inch of skin on the palm of your hands can contain as many as 3,000 sweat glands.

You probably also know that electricity travels more efficiently on wet surfaces than on dry surfaces. Thus, one way to determine how much a person is sweating is to see how well the surface of his or her skin can conduct an electrical current. This is the idea behind galvanic skin response. To measure it, researchers attach electrodes to a person's skin and then pass a low-voltage electrical current between the electrodes. They are looking to find changes in the skin's ability to conduct that current, which are often associated with different kinds of stimuli that the researchers would introduce to the person.
For example, galvanic skin response is one of three physiological tests that make up the polygraph, or lie-detector test. Most people feel nervous when they lie, particularly when lying to the police or other authorities, because of the risks of being caught in the lie. As you know, people sweat more when they are nervous. Thus, a galvanic skin response test can be used to determine whether a suspect sweats more when being asked incriminating questions (e.g., "did you commit this crime?") than when being asked questions that the interrogator already knows the answer to (e.g., "what is your name?") The change in perspiration is not big enough to be observed by the naked eye; however, by seeing whether the skin conducts an electrical current more efficiently while a person is answering one question versus another, researchers and interrogators gain one clue as to the truthfulness of the person's statements.

Pupil Dilation

The pupil is the darkest and centermost circle observed when looking at the eye. During waking hours, it dilates (becomes wider) and contracts (becomes smaller) fairly constantly in order to regulate the amount of light coming into the eye. When you go from a dark environment into a lighter one, your pupils immediately contract so that the increase in light won't damage your eyes. Conversely, when you go from a light environment into a darker one, your pupils will dilate in order to take in every bit of available light, so that you can see as clearly as possible. The pupil can dilate to around 8 to 9 mm, can contract to approximately 1.5 mm, and can react to a stimulus in about one-fifth of a second. **Pupillometry** is the practice of measuring changes in pupil dilation and contraction.

Although the pupil serves a regulatory function by controlling the intake of light, pupil dilation and contraction are also affected by a number of other things. These include emotional arousal, the use of stimulants or depressants, and the distance of one's object of focus. Pupil size is also affected by our level of attraction to what we are seeing. When you look at an attractive person, for instance, your pupils dilate. And, as we will discuss in more detail below, having larger pupils also makes us more attractive to other people.

Even though we can watch pupils dilate and contract with the naked eye, instruments that measure changes in pupil size in a more sophisticated way have been developed only within the last 30 years or so. The most commonly used device is called a video-based pupillometer; it observes the eye through a closed-circuit television system and uses a signal processor to measure changes in pupil size. (You might recall seeing this type of system used in the 2003 movie, *The Recruit.*) Researchers measuring pupil size in this way often use a technique called **task-evoked pupillary response** to measure how pupil dilation changes in response to a specific stimulus.

Heart rate, blood pressure, skin temperature, galvanic skin response, and pupil dilation are not the only markers of nervous system activity. However, they are among the most commonly measured markers, because they are relatively easy to identify and measure. Indeed, social scientists have looked at all five of these markers in research on human communication. In the next section, we will describe some examples of studies that have applied measurement of nervous system activity to the task of better understanding human communication. As in other chapters, the studies described in this section are illustrative; this is not an exhaustive review of all research done in each of these areas.

Applications to Human Communication

You can probably already think of numerous ways in which nervous system activity might affect, or be affected by, communication. Consider the last time you got into a heated argument with someone. Of course, you were thinking about your position and points you wanted to make, but your body was probably reacting in several other ways on its own. Your heart probably started to beat faster than normal and your blood pressure probably went up. It's quite likely that your skin temperature also increased, which could have caused you to perspire more.

These are all examples of adaptive responses. When your body perceives some type of challenge or threat – like it would when you are getting into a heated argument with someone – it deals with that situation by activating the sympathetic nervous system. Your heart rate and blood pressure go up in order to provide your brain, other organs, and muscles with an increased blood supply, so that you have more energy if you need it to deal with the challenge. Your skin temperature goes up because your body directs blood *away* from other parts of your body that aren't essential at the time and *toward* your muscles and skin tissue. As a result, you perspire more than usual, so that your body won't overheat. When the perceived challenge or threat is done, these activities subside and your body goes back into its normal operating mode.

A number of researchers have studied nervous system activity and the ways in which it affects, and is affected by, communication and relational processes. In this section, we describe some of these studies and the results they have produced. As in the previous section, we have divided our discussion among five markers of nervous system activity: heart rate, blood pressure, skin temperature, galvanic skin response, and pupil dilation. We conclude this section with a short note about some of the topics that researchers in this area might consider in the future.

Applications with Heart Rate

One of the most promising lines of research examining heart rate has been in the area of marital communication. John Gottman, a social psychologist at the University of Washington, studies marital conflict and the ways in which spouses react to conflict physiologically. Much of his work has demonstrated two important patterns with respect to heart rate. First, the quality of people's marriages is associated with how much their heart rates change in response to conflict; and second, this pattern is different for women than for men. In some of their early research with spouses, for instance, Levenson and Gottman (1985) discovered that marital partners' heart rate, when they were engaged in conflict and when they were discussing the events of the day, predicted decreases in their marital satisfaction three years later – but this was only true for husbands. In particular, husbands' decreases in marital satisfaction three years after the study were predicted by their heart rates during an events-of-the-day conversation and by their heart rates during a conflict episode. For wives, however, this was not the case.

In other research, which is described in Gottman (1994), Gottman has discovered that husbands' heart rates during conflict episodes and events-of-the-day discussions could distinguish between husbands whose wives were seriously considering divorce three years later and those whose wives were not. Interestingly, husbands whose wives were *not* seriously considering divorce three years after the study had had higher heart rates during both types of conversations. In fact, heart rates for the husbands in the two groups differed from each other by an average of 20.11 beats per minute, which is remarkable, given that most laboratory studies produce differences in heart rate that average less than five beats per minute.

Applications with Blood Pressure

As with heart rate, a number of studies have looked at blood pressure during conversations between spouses. In one such study, Brown and Smith (1992) looked at 45 couples' attempts to persuade each other. They found that husbands' systolic blood pressure increased sharply immediately before and during their attempts to persuade their wives. Wives, on the other hand, did not show elevated blood pressure levels (see also Smith & Brown, 1991).

In another study, Denton, Burleson, Hobbs, Von Stein, and Rodriguez (2001) measured blood pressure reactivity in 120 participants, (comprising 60 married couples), whom the researchers had classified as being either *initiators* of relationship problem discussions or *avoiders* of such discussions. The participants went through a number of laboratory activities that were designed to raise their stress levels. Denton and his team found a number of differences with respect to blood pressure. First, as they had expected, people who avoided talking about their relationship problems (whether male or female) had greater reactivity in systolic blood pressure than did people who generally initiated relationship problem discussions. Moreover, husbands whose wives were "avoiders" showed greater systolic and diastolic blood pressure reactivity than did husbands whose wives were "initiators." Blood pressure reactivity was especially high for initiator husbands who were married to avoider wives.

One of the more surprising findings in the Denton et al. study was that husbands had lower levels of systolic and diastolic blood pressure reactivity than did women. Other studies have found just the opposite, for both systolic blood pressure (Lawler, Wilcox, & Anderson, 1995) and diastolic blood pressure (Murphy, Stoney, Alpert, & Walker, 1995). In line with other research (e.g., Eichorn, 1970), however, Denton and colleagues found that blood pressure measures taken at the beginning of the study were higher for men than for women.

Applications with Skin Temperature

One area in which skin temperature has been studied is that of emotion. Psychologist Paul Ekman has proposed what he calls the **facial feedback hypothesis**. His prediction is that, by simply forming a facial expression (e.g., smiling) that is associated with an emotion (e.g., happiness), a person will begin to experience the physiological markers associated with that emotion. People who work in service industries are often taught that, if they just force themselves to smile, they will actually begin feeling better – if this has ever happened to you, then you have an understanding of what Ekman is proposing. In his research (e.g., Ekman, Levenson, & Friesen, 1983; Levenson, Ekman, & Friesen, 1990), Ekman asked some professional actors to form facial expressions associated with various emotions (e.g., making a "sad face," a "scared face," or an "angry face). While they were doing so, Ekman measured their physiological processes and compared them to instances when the participants were actually experiencing those same emotions. Ekman discovered, among other things, that making an "angry face" caused his participants' skin temperatures to rise, and that making a "sad face" caused their skin temperatures to fall. Surprisingly, making a "happy face" did not change participants' skin temperature at all.

Other research has looked at how people's skin temperature changes during actual interactions with others. In one study, Le Poire and Burgoon (1996) asked college students to have conversations with **confederates** who were trained to display high or low levels of nonverbal involvement in the conversation. The researchers looked to see whether the students' skin temperatures would change as a result of the confederates' behaviors. After the start of each conversation, the confederates began to display either very high involvement, high involvement, low involvement, or very low involvement, by manipulation nonverbal behaviors such as eye contact, forward lean, and direct body orientation. Le Poire and Burgoon discovered that the students' skin temperatures increased in response to *all four types of involvement change.* That is, no matter how the confederates changed their behaviors, the students' skin temperatures went up. This may be a function of the students having become psychologically aroused by the changes in confederates' conversational style.

Applications with Galvanic Skin Response

Like skin temperature, galvanic skin response is a marker of sympathetic nervous system arousal and it shows a number of connections with emotion. In a pair of studies, for example, Kring and Gordon (1998) had participants watch film clips that were designed to highlight and elicit different types of emotions. While they were watching, the participants' galvanic skin response was being measured. Kring and Gordon looked at sex differences in the responses and found that men had greater reactivity than women while watching films what were meant to make them angry or fearful. Women, by contrast, had greater reactivity than men while watching films that were designed to make them sad or disgusted. Other studies have also demonstrated the effects of emotion on galvanic skin response (see, e.g., Geen & Rakosky, 1973).

Other research has linked galvanic skin response to patterns of family communication. In one study, Wiesenfeld, Malatesta, Whitman, Granrose, and Uili (1985) looked at mother-infant attachment. They had two groups of mothers: those who breast-fed their infants and those who bottle-fed them. The researchers compared the physiological responses of these two groups of mothers to their infants' emotional signals. Mothers in both groups watched videotapes of their own infants' emotional expressions (crying, smiling, and emotionally neutral displays); while watching, the mothers' galvanic skin response was being monitored. The researchers found that breast-feeding mothers had lower galvanic skin response and also lower heart rates than did the bottle-feeding mothers. Why is this the case? Andreassi (2000) speculated that hormones released in women during lactation might help to dampen general autonomic nervous system arousal and increase relaxation during feeding, and that these may help to facilitate mother-infant attachment. We will discuss this issue in greater detail in the next chapter.

In their research with married couples, Levenson and Gottman (1983, 1985) also discovered that both husbands' and wives' galvanic skin response during conflict episodes and conversations about daily events in 1980 predicted decreases in their marital satisfaction three years later. (The average correlations between galvanic skin response and the declines in marital satisfaction were .48 for husbands and .62 for wives.)

Applications with Pupillometry

We have already noted that pupil sizes change when the available light changes, when we feel emotionally aroused, and when we use stimulants or depressants. More interestingly for communication researchers, however, is that the sympathetic nervous system also causes pupils to dilate when we look at attractive people (Aboyoun & Dabbs, 1998). Specifically, pupil dilation is involved in interpersonal attraction and pair bonding, in two interrelated ways. First, our pupils dilate when we look at someone we find physically and/or sexually attractive (Andersen, Todd-Mancillas, & DiClemente, 1980). In one study, Aboyoun and Dabbs (1998) had people look at images of clothed and nude adults. They found that their participants' pupils dilated more in response to nude images, *regardless of the sex of the participants or the sex of the person in the photo.* Second, having dilated pupils makes us more physically attractive to other people, other things being equal (Hess, 1975). In fact, in earlier times, women used to put a substance called *belladonna* in their eyes, which would make their eyes dilate. *Belladonna* means, literally, "beautiful woman," and the idea was that having larger pupils would make the women more attractive to others.

You may have noticed an interesting parallel between these two ideas. For example, a man's pupils dilate if he finds a particular woman attractive, and she therefore finds him more attractive because his pupils are dilated. This causes her pupils to dilate, which causes him to be more attracted to her, and so on. In this way, pupil dilation can be thought of as an adaptive response that helps people attract potential romantic partners. Some studies have also found that pupils dilate in response to sounds. In one study, Dabbs (1997) had people listen to "sexually charged" sounds and found that this caused pupil dilation, especially in people who had high levels of testosterone.

Future Applications

Because they are all associated with autonomic nervous system arousal, changes in heart rate, blood pressure, skin temperature, galvanic skin response, and pupil size could be related to a number of communicative processes, some of which have been studied and many of which have not. For instance, the type of physiological arousal that engaged or newlywed couples experience when talking about their relationships might predict their long-term happiness and satisfaction. Physiological reactivity during parent-child conflict may also be related not only with the quality of the parent-child relationship but also with the parent's mental health or the child's success in his or her adult relationships. Galvanic skin response during conversations between college friends could be related to their likelihood of staying in contact with each other after graduation. These are all speculations based on what we know about these physiological markers, but they illustrate some of the many ways in which knowledge about the nervous system can help us to better understand the ways that people communicate in their relationships.

Key Terms

Arteries
Autonomic nervous system
BPM (beats per minute)
Capillaries
Catecholamines
Central nervous system
Confederate
Diastolic blood pressure
Eccrine sweat gland
Epinephrine
Facial feedback hypothesis
Finger photoplethysmography
IBI (interbeat interval)
Korotkoff sound
Neuron
Neurotransmitters
Norepinephrine
Parasympathetic nervous system
Peripheral nervous system
Pupillometry
Reflexes
Skin conductance
Somatic nervous system
Sphygmomanometer
Sympathetic nervous system
Synapse
Systolic blood pressure
Task-evoked pupillary response
Thermistor probes
Thermoregulation
Veins

Chapter Four: The Endocrine System

Most everyone knows that behavior is sometimes affected by hormones. Exactly *how*, though, is often a mystery – but one we will begin to unravel in this chapter. Hormones are controlled by the endocrine system, a large and complex collection of glands located throughout the body that work together to respond to our various needs. For instance, some glands get activated when we get stressed out; others are activated when it's time for us to sleep; and still others are activated when we're sexually aroused.

In this chapter, we will look first at the structure and function of the endocrine system. Although it includes a number of different glands, we will focus only on a few. Next, we'll discuss the process of measuring a person's hormone levels, and finally, we'll survey some of the research that has linked specific hormones to communicative behavior.

Structure and Function of the Endocrine System

What, exactly, is a **hormone**? The easiest way to think of hormones is as chemical messengers. They are produced by **glands**, which are organs of the endocrine system, and are carried by the bloodstream to various other cells or organs of the body. Even though hormones are carried by the blood to all parts of the body, however, a given hormone can only affect particular cells or organs that have receptors to which the hormone can attach. These are called **target cells** or **target organs**. If a cell or organ does not have receptors for a given hormone, that hormone cannot act on that cell or organ.

There are several different hormones in your body, but nearly all of them can be classified as belonging to one of two groups. Some are made of *amino acid-based molecules*, such as proteins, amines, or peptides. These include, among others, oxytocin, growth hormone, melatonin, and insulin. Other hormones are *steroids*, which are derived from cholesterol. These include, among others, cortisol, testosterone, estrogens, and progesterone.

Once they attach, or *bind*, with a cell or organ, hormones act by either increasing or decreasing the metabolic process. In fact, the word *hormone* is derived from a Greek term meaning "to arouse" – and in a sense, that's what hormones do to cells or organs. Amino acid-based hormones bind to receptors located on the plasma membrane surrounding a cell. By contrast, steroid hormones break through the plasma membrane and actually enter the cell, where they bind with receptors located inside the cell.

The endocrine system is made up of a number of different glands. For our purposes, it is not necessary to review them all – instead, we have selected a few of the more important glands to describe below.

Major Glands of the Endocrine System

In this section, we will identify and describe some of the major glands of the endocrine system, including the pituitary, adrenal, and pineal glands, the gonads, and the hypothalamus. We will locate and describe the purpose of each gland and then identify the discuss the hormones that each gland produces. More detailed discussion of some of these hormones can be found in the "applications" section at the end of this chapter.

The **pituitary gland** is located in the brain, close to the hypothalamus. It is about the size of a grape, and it has two different sections, or lobes: the **anterior pituitary** and the **posterior pituitary**. The anterior pituitary releases six different hormones. **Growth hormone** causes amino acids to be built into proteins and causes cells to grow and divide so that bones and muscles will grow. **Prolactin** is a hormone with a structure similar to growth hormone; its job is to stimulate milk production in lactating women. **Adrenocorticotropic hor-**

mone (ACTH) regulates part of the adrenal gland and helps to stimulate the release of **cortisol**, which we will discuss in greater detail below. **Thyrotropic hormone** influences the activity of the thyroid gland. In females, **follicle-stimulating hormone** stimulates the development of **follicles** in the ovaries, which consist of a developing egg surrounded by cells. In men, follicle-stimulating hormone stimulates the development of sperm by the testes. Finally, **luteinizing hormone** triggers ovulation in women and leads to the production of **progesterone**. In men, luteinizing hormone stimulates the production of testosterone.

In a technical sense, the posterior pituitary is not really an endocrine gland because it does not *produce* the hormones that it releases. Instead, it stores two hormones that are produced by neurons in the hypothalamus and releases them into the bloodstream when necessary. **Oxytocin** is a hormone that is best known for the roles it plays in childbirth. It stimulates contractions of the uterine muscles to initiate delivery of an unborn baby, and it is released in significant amounts when women breast-feed. As we note below, oxytocin appears to calm, relax, and reduce pain in women during childbirth and breastfeeding. Importantly, both men and women release oxytocin during sexual climax, when it may help to reinforce feelings of love and attachment. A second hormone released by the posterior pituitary is **antidiuretic hormone**, which is also known as **vasopressin**. When bodies produce urine, vasopressin directs the kidneys to absorb more of the water from the urine than they otherwise would, which reduces the overall amount of urine produced. As we discuss below, vasopressin also appears to have some of the same pain- and stress-reducing effects as oxytocin.

The **adrenal glands** are two bean-shaped organs that curve over the top of the kidneys. Like the pituitary gland, an adrenal gland has two separate parts: the **adrenal cortex** and the **adrenal medulla**. The adrenal cortex produces three types of hormones. **Mineralocorticoids** regulate the mineral content of blood. In particular, they make sure that the blood supply does not contain too many or too few sodium or potassium ions. **Glucocorticoids** regulate cell metabolism and help the body deal with stress. One type of glucocorticoid that we will discuss in more detail below is cortisol, which is also known as

hydrocortisone. Finally, the adrenal cortex produces small quantities of the male and female **sex hormones**, including **androgens** (the male sex hormones) and **estrogens** (the female sex hormones).

In the previous chapter, we discussed the roles of two catecholamines: epinephrine and norepinephrine. These are released by the adrenal medulla, and they have the effect of helping to prepare the body for the "fight-or-flight" response that comes with exposure to some type of stressor.

The **pineal gland** is a cone-shaped gland located in the brain. The only hormone that it appears to produce in significant amounts is **melatonin**. Melatonin is responsible for the drowsy, sleepy feeling we get at night. It is sometimes referred to as the "sleep trigger," because it is released in the greatest concentrations at night, when it induces us to sleep. It is at its lowest level around the middle of the day, when most of us feel wide awake. When people travel long distances through different times zones, they often have trouble adopting a normal sleeping pattern because their pineal glands are releasing melatonin according to their normal body clocks: thus, they may be drowsy at 2 p.m. and wide awake at 2 a.m.!

The **gonads** are the glands that produce the male and female sex hormones. Female gonads, called **ovaries**, produce two types of hormones. Although people sometimes refer to estrogen as a single hormone, it is actually a class of hormones that includes **estrone** and **estradiol**, among others. These lead to the development of **secondary sex characteristics** in females, such as the development of the breasts and reproductive organs and the stimulation of pubic hair. Estrogens also play important roles in preparing the body for pregnancy and lactation. The ovaries also produce progesterone, which works with estrogens to cause women to have regular menstrual cycles. In pregnant women, it also works to prevent spontaneous abortion and helps prepare the breast tissues for lactation.

The male gonads are the **testes**, or testicles, which are suspended in the scrotum. The testes produce sperm, which are actually cells rather than hormones. They also produce a class of hormones called androgens, of which **testosterone** is the most important. Testosterone causes men to develop secondary sex characteristics, such as facial hair, lower voices, and larger muscles, and it also causes the male reproductive system to mature. Testosterone is also necessary for the continuous production of sperm. When a man's testosterone level drops significantly, he becomes sterile. Doctors often prescribe testosterone injections to treat such cases.

The hypothalamus is actually part of the central nervous system rather than the endocrine system. However, it plays an important role in the endocrine system because it produces releasing and inhibiting hormones that act on the anterior pituitary gland. Releasing hormone stimulates the anterior pituitary to secrete various hormones into the bloodstream; inhibiting hormone shuts those secretions off. In addition, as we noted above, neurons in the hypothalamus produce oxytocin and antidiuretic hormone, which are then sent to the posterior pituitary gland for storage and eventual release.

Measuring Endocrine System Activity

In the previous chapter, we discussed the process of measuring nervous system activity. This discussion included a number of different "markers," each of which required a different strategy for measuring. In some ways, the measurement of hormonal activity is simpler, by comparison. That's because nearly every hormone can be measured in bodily fluids such as saliva or blood. However, as we will discuss in this section, handling bodily fluids can be risky and should only be done by trained researchers taking proper safety precautions.

Before we address *how* to measure hormones, let us first discuss *what* to measure. Two issues, in particular, have been important to social scientists with respect to the effects of hormones: basal hormone level and hormone reactivity.

What We Measure About Hormones

Let's imagine that you wanted to study the effects of testosterone on communication behaviors. One way to do so would be to look at how communication behaviors are related to a person's normal, everyday level of testosterone. This is what researchers refer to as the *basal level*, and it is often calculated as the average of several measures taken of the hormone over a period of time. (As we will discuss below, it is often necessary to take several measurements since the levels of many hormones fluctuate systematically through the day and night; see Gorman & Lee, 2002; Richardson & Martin, 1988.)

In a study of testosterone levels in married and unmarried men, for instance, Gray, Kahlenberg, Barrett, Lipson, and Ellison (2002) took four measurements of testosterone from each participant, two in the morning and two in the evening. They then averaged the four measurements to arrive at each participant's basal testosterone level. As predicted, they found that basal testosterone was significantly higher in unmarried than in married men (see also Ellison, Lipson, & Meredith, 1989).

A second way to look at the effects of testosterone would be to see how much a person's testosterone level changes in reaction to something. The size and direction of the change in a person's hormone level as a result of being exposed to some stimulus is called the person's *hormonal reactivity*. Studying reactivity requires taking a baseline measurement, which is a measurement taken prior to exposing the person to a stimulus. Additional measurements are taken during and after exposure to the stimulus, and these measurements are compared to the baseline to determine the level of reactivity.

For example, Turner, Altemus, Enos, Cooper, and McGuinness (1999) measured levels of the oxytocin in a group of adult women before, during, and after mental imagery tasks and massage. By looking at how much the participants' oxytocin levels changed before, during, and after each stimulus, the researchers were able to discover how much hormonal reactivity each activity caused. The study found that women's oxytocin levels went up when the women were being massaged, went down when the women were made to feel negative emotions, and showed no reaction when the women were made to feel positive emotions.

Nearly every social science study investigating the effects of hormones looks at one or both of these two issues. Now that we know what to look for, let us discuss the methods that researchers use to measure the hormones themselves.

How Hormones are Measured

To measure basal hormone levels or hormonal reactivity, researchers must do two things: collect appropriate samples of bodily fluids, and then analyze those samples for their concentrations of the hormones being studied. As we noted above, sample collection is not complicated but it does require the use of specific materials, a working knowledge of what influences the hormone being measured, and the enforcement of certain safety measures (see Grunberg & Singer, 1990).

Collecting samples. First, researchers must know which bodily fluids the hormone of interest will be found in. Some hormones, like cortisol or testosterone, can be measured from blood or saliva (Baum & Grunberg, 1995), and there is a good deal of consistency between these types of measurements (Kirschbaum & Hellhammer, 1989, 1994; Navarro, Juan, & Bonnin, 1986). When studying these types of hormones, researchers often prefer taking saliva samples. Compared to blood samples, salivary samples are less invasive for participants and are simpler because they do not require much in the way of special training for the researcher.

Saliva samples are often taken using a receptacle called a salivette (Sarstedt, Inc.), which looks at first like a plastic test tube. The salivette contains a small piece of cotton that the participant is asked to chew on and to saturate with his or her saliva. Afterward, the cotton is placed inside a small plastic container that has a tiny hole in one end. A cap is placed on the other end of the container to hold the cotton inside, and then this entire assembly is placed inside a plastic test tube. (See Figure 4.1.) Usually, the tubes are then frozen until analysis so that the saliva won't begin to mold.

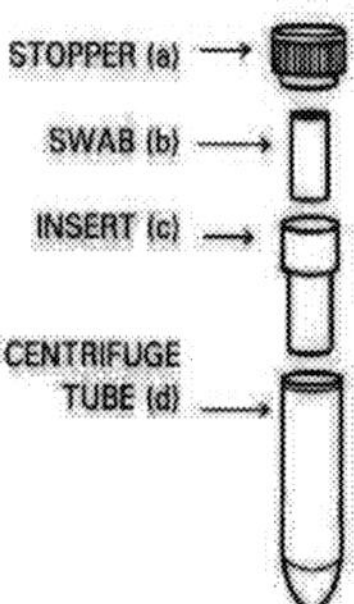

Figure 4.1: The Salivette

Before analysis, the salivettes are thawed and then spun in a **centrifuge**. This draws the saliva out of the cotton through the tiny hole in the small container and into the larger test tube. The analysis of some hormones is actually contaminated by the cotton in a salivette. In those cases, saliva samples are usually taken using polystyrene tubes. A researcher would have participants expectorate through a straw that leads into the tube, and then seal the tubes with the saliva inside. It is recommended that the researcher wear latex gloves while taking and handling the samples, but more sophisticated safety measures are not usually required.

Besides the fact that they are simple and noninvasive, using saliva samples is advantageous because it allows researchers to collect the samples in non-laboratory settings. Since salivettes are small and easy to use, the researcher can use them in field experiments and observational studies, and can even train people to take their own saliva samples over a period of time, allowing for data collections in people's own homes.

Other hormones, such as oxytocin or vasopressin, must be measured using blood samples. As you might imagine, this requires much greater attention to safety. Blood should only be drawn by a licensed nurse or **phlebotomist**. Before they take blood samples as a part of a study, researchers must make certain that their laboratories are properly equipped and that everyone working on the study has been trained in appropriate safety measures.

Hormones like oxytocin can be analyzed either in **serum** or **plasma**. You may know that if you let blood sit for a period of time, it will begin to *coagulate*, or clot. The fluid that is left over is serum. Similarly, if you put tubes of blood into a centrifuge and spin them at high speed, the blood will begin to separate. The various cells found in the blood will be drawn to the bottom of the tubes, and the upper part of the tubes will contain a yellowish liquid made up of water, electrolytes, proteins, and other substances. This is plasma. Researchers must be aware of which substance is to be analyzed for hormone levels when they are designing their studies.

As we mentioned, studies of hormonal reactivity typically require that several samples of bodily fluid be taken so that changes in the levels of the hormone can be seen. This is fine if the measurement is being done with saliva, but most people don't want to be stuck with a needle several times within a short period! In these cases, nurses or phlebotomists may use a device called an **indwelling catheter**, which is inserted into the arm like a syringe and then stays there for the duration of the study. Using an indwelling catheter, a nurse or phlebotomist can take multiple blood draws without repeated **venipuncture**.
As we noted above, researchers should familiarize themselves with things – besides the activities in a study – that affect the levels of the hormones they are interested in studying. These can include, among other things, exercise, food consumption, and the use of caffeine, alcohol, or tobacco (see Denton et al., 2001). Some hormones also follow a **diurnal rhythm**, which means they are present at higher levels during certain times of the day than during other times and the pattern is relatively consistent from day to day (Nelson, 2000). To make up for this ebb and flow, researchers may schedule all of their data collections during the same time each day. Some hormones are also affected by the use of prescription medicines, including birth control pills. An **endocrinologist** may use screening questionnaires to determine whether potential participants are using any drugs that would affect their hormone measurements, and such people may be excluded from taking part in their studies.

Analyzing samples. Once the appropriate saliva or blood samples have been collected, they must be analyzed for the levels of the hormones being studied. The tests used to determine hormone level are called assays. We do not go into great detail here about the conduct of assays, because few communication researchers have either the technical expertise or the necessary facilities and equipment to perform these analyses themselves. Instead, they may make arrangements with a laboratory that is equipped to do the analyses on a fee basis. These labs may be found at large research universities, particularly in their medical schools or in their departments of endocrinology, biopsychology, or kinesiology. Others are professional laboratories that are used by medical personnel as well as social scientists. The laboratory doing the assays will advise the researcher on how to store and ship samples for analysis. Proper care must be exercised, both to keep the researchers and laboratory technicians safe and to prevent the fluid samples from spoiling.

In this section, we have briefly described the process of collecting and analyzing bodily fluid samples for research on hormone levels. What can such research tell us about human communication? In the following section, we discuss a small handful of hormones that have been studied for their connections to communication in human relationships. As before, this list is illustrative, not exhaustive, but it will give you some idea of why social science researchers have been – and should be – interested in the endocrine system,

Applications to Human Communication

The endocrine system produces a number of hormones, only a few of which have been studied in relation to communicative processes. These include cortisol, testosterone, oxytocin, dopamine, and endogenous opioid peptides. In this section, we will briefly discuss research on each of these hormones and suggest ways in which they can help illuminate the process of human communication. We will close the section with a short discussion on future potential applications of this type of research.

Cortisol

Cortisol is a steroid hormone that is produced and secreted by the adrenal cortex in response to the release of corticotropic releasing hormone (CRH) by the hypothalamus. Cortisol is sometimes referred to as the "stress hormone" because it is released in response to physical, mental, or emotional stress. The secretion of cortisol causes a breakdown of muscle protein, which leads to the release of amino acids into the bloodstream. These amino acids are used by the liver to synthesize glucose for energy. Cortisol also depresses systems of the body that are not essential during stressful situations, such as the digestive and reproductive systems. It plays a dual role with the immune system: it stimulates immune organs in case the body must deal with injury, yet it also suppresses the immune system to prevent it from overreacting to injury and needlessly damaging tissues. In these ways, cortisol equips the body (much like ANS arousal) to deal with stress in the short term (McEwan, 1999; Nelson, 2000; Sapolsky, 2000). Chronically high levels of cortisol are very damaging to the body in the long term, however, because cortisol suppresses the immune system and inhibits bone formation (see Porterfield, 2001).

A number of studies have demonstrated that cortisol levels rise when people are faced with stress-evoking stimuli. In a typical example, Kiecolt-Glaser, Malarkey, Chee, Newton, Cacioppo, Mao, and Glaser (1993) took baseline measurements of cortisol from a group of married adults and then induced participants to engage in a 30-minute marital conflict. They found that wives showed greater increases in cortisol secretion during the conflict when their husbands disengaged from the conflict than when they did not. Husbands' hormone levels, by contrast, were not affected by the conflict episode. Other studies, such as Grossi, Åhs, and Lundberg (1998), have used a series of stress-inducing activities, including a cold pressor test, a mental math test, and a stroop color word test (a timed test that presents participants with names of colors that are spelled out in letters of a different color – the word "yellow" appearing in blue letters, for instance – wherein participants must identify the color of the letters in rapid succession). Both men and women in the Grossi et al. study showed significant increases in their cortisol levels after the stressful activities, with men showing a larger increase than women (for other examples, see Bassett, Marshall, & Spilane, 1987; Stahl & Dorner, 1982).

One obvious application of cortisol measurement to the understanding of family communication is in the area of marital conflict. Some investigations have shown that conflict episodes between spouses, because they are typically stressful events, elicit cortisol secretion. In a laboratory study, Miller, Dopp, Myers, Stevens, and Fahey (1999) had spouses engage in a 15-minute discussion about a marital problem and measured their cortisol levels before and after the conversations. They also measured the amount of cynical hostility being displayed during the interactions and found that, for men who displayed a high amount of cynical hostility, anger in the conversations was associated with elevated cortisol levels, but that this was not true for men who displayed low amounts of cynical hostility. Moreover, Kiecolt-Glaser, Newton, Cacioppo, MacCallum, Glaser, and Malarkey (1996) studied the cortisol levels of newlywed spouses by taking hourly measurements over the course of a day in which the couples had engaged in some type of conflict. They found that wives' cortisol levels were significantly elevated when their new husbands withdrew from marital conflict.

There is also reason to believe that spouses' levels of cortisol reactivity may be related to the quality of their relationship or its communication style. After videotaping 80 couples engaging in conflict and classifying the couples as having either predominantly positive communication behaviors, predominantly negative communication behaviors, or asymmetric behaviors (one spouse is predominantly positive; the other, predominantly negative), Fehm-Wolfsdorf, Groth, Kaiser, and Hahlweg (1999) reported that couples with predominantly positive communication behaviors showed significantly greater increases in cortisol during the conflict episode than did the couples with predominantly negative communication behaviors. This suggests, perhaps, that cortisol reactivity to marital conflict is associated with the quality of the relationship, with spouses in higher-quality relationships showing greater stress reactivity to conflict than do those in relationships of lesser quality (see also, e.g., Kiecolt-Glaser et al., 1993). This is one of many interesting points with respect to conflict in marriages (or other family subsystems) that awaits attention from family communication scholars.

Testosterone

Testosterone, which is sometimes referred to as the "male sex hormone" even though it is present in both sexes, is an androgen steroid hormone secreted by the testes and adrenal cortex (Nelson, 2000). It stimulates muscle development, hair growth, and the production of sperm in men, and has also been linked to male competition and aggression in both humans and animals (for review, see Archer, 1994).

Several studies have linked men's testosterone levels to changes in marital and parental status. Booth and Dabbs (1993), in a study of over 4,000 servicemen, reported that participants' basal testosterone levels were inversely associated with their likelihood of marrying, and, for those participants who did marry, testosterone levels were directly associated with their likelihood of engaging in extramarital sex. Gray et al. (2002) found that testosterone levels were significantly higher in unmarried men than in married men, even after controlling for the effects of age, and Mazur and Michalek (1998) found that men's testosterone levels were highest four to eight years prior to marriage and began to decline shortly after marriage.

Testosterone levels appear to drop in men not only when they marry but again when they become fathers. Storey, Walsh, Quinton, and Wynne-Edwards (2002) compared the testosterone levels of men whose wives had given birth within the previous three weeks to those of men whose wives were due to give birth in three weeks or less, and found that men in the former group had 33% lower testosterone levels than did those in the latter group. Storey et al. also reported that engaging in pseudo-parental behaviors, such as holding a baby doll, decreased testosterone levels in their participants. Berg and Wynne-Edwards (2001) similarly found that testosterone levels were lower in men who were expecting the birth of their first child than they were for controls.

These researchers have speculated that such changes in men's basal testosterone levels at the points of marriage and fatherhood facilitate decreases in aggressive, competitive tendencies that may have been more adaptive before these turning points than afterward. When seeking a mate, for instance, men are in competition with other men, and testosterone may facilitate their ability to compete (see Mazur & Booth, 1998). After finding a mate, however, the need for such competition (and thus for a high level of testosterone) is reduced, theoretically. Likewise, from an evolutionary perspective, testosterone may contribute to a level of vigilance (and, if necessary, aggression) in men that is required to reduce the likelihood that other men will copulate with their mates and to increase men's likelihood of producing offspring of their own. After men produce children, however, their tendencies toward aggression may become maladaptive, and their further decreases in testosterone may lead to more nurturant behaviors.

Oxytocin

Oxytocin is a peptide hormone that is produced in the hypothalamus and released into the circulatory system via the pituitary gland. It is perhaps best known for the two important functions that it serves with respect to childbirth: it initiates the delivery process by stimulating uterine contractions, and is responsible for the let-down reflex, stimulating milk ejection in lactating women (Becker & Breedlove, 2002). Oxytocin is also secreted during sexual interaction and appears to play a role in making sex rewarding. Several investigations have indicated that oxytocin is released into the circulatory systems of both men and women at sexual orgasm (Carmichael, Humbert, Dixen, Palmisano, Greenleaf, & Davidson, 1987; Murphy, Seckl, Burton, Checkley, & Lightman, 1990; Richard, Moos, & Freund-Mercier, 1991). Moreover, the amount of oxytocin released into the bloodstream is related to the subjective intensity of orgasm, at least for women (Carmichael, Warburton, Dixen, & Davidson, 1994). It is also elicited by touch and massage, even when the touch is nonsexual (Turner et al., 1999).

A number of researchers have commented on a provocative parallel that exists with respect to oxytocin. First, it is produced by the body at relationally significant moments; that is, the events that cause oxytocin secretion are significant in terms of relational bonding and attachment. For instance, it is produced at sexual climax, which is important for the maintenance of pair bonds (Carmichael et al., 1987), and it is produced in women when they deliver and nurse their babies, which is important for parent-child attachment (Becker & Breedlove, 2002). There is also evidence that oxytocin release is associated with flirting behavior, which is often a precursor to the formation of pair bonds (see Carter, 1992). Second, it makes people feel good. It promotes relaxation, lowers the heart rate, and inhibits stress (Altemus, Deuster, Carter, & Gold, 1995; Amico, Johnston, & Vagnucci, 1994;

Carter & Altemus, 1997; Chiodera, Salvarani, Bacchi-Modena, Spallanzani, Cigarini, Alboni, Gardini, & Coiro, 1991). It is even thought to be responsible for the "afterglow" effect that couples experience after lovemaking (Arletti, Benelli, & Bertolini, 1992).

Taken together, these two observations suggest that oxytocin plays a critical role in bonding and attachment processes, both in humans and in other mammals. Simply put, it may be an important part of the brain's reward system, the neurological function that promotes behaviors that are important to survival and reproduction by making people feel good when they engage in those behaviors. Panksepp has written extensively on the connections between oxytocin and human attachment (see, e.g., Nelson & Panksepp, 1998; Panksepp, 1998). He suggested that "A straightforward emotional prediction is that brain oxytocin may evoke warm positive feelings of social strength and comfort when aroused by peripheral stimuli" (Panksepp, 1992, p. 243; see also Insel, 1997). Similarly, Porges's polyvagal theory (1995, 1996, 1997, 1998) offers that oxytocin release can facilitate a conditioning process that can help explain why friendship and parent-child bonding are so important and why people grieve to the extent that they do when they experience the loss of loved ones (for additional examples, see Taylor, 2002; Uvnäs-Moberg, 1998).

The connections between oxytocin and psychological and communicological processes have not been widely studied. On the basis of theory and other existing research on oxytocin, however, one might predict that the secretion of oxytocin (especially during relationally significant events) is a part of what makes love, and loving relationships, such as close family relationships, rewarding. It may be part of the reason why being in love feels so good, both emotionally and physically. This is a product of the endocrine system that is ripe for relationship research.

Dopamine

Dopamine is a hormone that is released in the nucleus accumbens (an area of the forebrain) and is involved in a number of important human functions, such as attention, learning, and movement. Like oxytocin, dopamine also works to create feelings of pleasure associated with various stimuli. In fact, quite a bit of research on dopamine has focused on its relationship to various forms of addiction (see Damsma, Day, & Fibiger, 1989; Samson, Hodge, Tolliver, & Haraguchi, 1993). Some studies have also suggested that dopamine plays a role in sexual interaction. In particular, it is thought to contribute to the reward level of sexual arousal, as opposed to sexual climax (see Larsson & Ahlenius, 1986). Much of the research on dopamine and sexual behavior has been conducted on animals, rather than on humans. In one such study, Damsma, Pfaus, Wenkstern, Phillips, and Fibiger (1992) found that, in male rats, more dopamine was released during foreplay than during the act of copulation itself (see also Pfaus, Damsma, Nomikos, Wenkstern, Blaha, Phillips, & Fibiger, 1990).

Other research suggests that social contact among prairie voles (which, like humans, are usually monogamous) may be motivated by dopamine release (Cascio, Yu, Insel, & Wang, 1998). The possibility that dopamine plays a part in other types of interactions that contribute to human relationships awaits investigation, however.

Endogenous Opioids

You're probably familiar with endogenous opioids without even realizing it. Endogenous opioids are peptides that, like oxytocin and dopamine, impart pleasure and reward. They are called *opioids* because their physical effects are a lot like those of opiates such as morphine, which include the relief of pain and feelings of elation.

There are three types of endogenous opioids: endorphins, enkephalins, and dynorphins (Nelson, 2000). You've probably heard of endorphins before. They're produced when we exercise and are credited with producing the "runners' high": the sensation of energy and elevated mood that runners sometimes experience in the wake of a long run.

Like the hormones discussed above, endogenous opioids also appear to be involved in sexual pleasure (see, e.g., Davis, 1984). A study by Murphy, Checkley, Seckl, and Lightman (1990) found that, when they administered to men an endorphin antagonist (a drug that blocks the effects of endorphins when they are released), it affected their experiences at sexual climax. In particular, men who were given the antagonist had less arousal and pleasure at orgasm than did men who were given a placebo. Moreover, the men in the placebo group had a 362% increase in their oxytocin levels at orgasm (compared to baseline measures taken before sexual arousal). By contrast, those who had taken the endorphin antagonist showed *no increase* in oxytocin levels at orgasm. This research suggests that endorphins play an important role (at least for men) in making sex pleasurable.

Future Applications

The study of hormones in human communication and behavior is a relatively field, and it offers a great deal of promise for helping us to understand why we react to certain things in certain ways. For instance, we already know that marital conflict increases cortisol; researchers might therefore look to see what other kinds of interpersonal or relational stressors are involved in the endocrine stress response. We also know that oxytocin, dopamine, and endogenous opioids give us a sense of calm and well-being. Could it be that these hormones are part of the reason why being in love feels so good? These and other possibilities await researchers in this area.

Key Terms

Adrenal cortex
Adrenal glands
Adrenal medulla
Adrenocorticotropic hormone (ACTH)
Androgens
Anterior pituitary lobe
Antidiuretic hormone
Centrifuge
Cortisol
Diurnal rhythm
Endocrinologist
Estradiol
Estrogens
Estrone
Follicles
Follicle-stimulating hormone
Gland
Glucocorticoids
Gonads
Growth hormone
Hormone
Hydrocortisone
Indwelling catheter
Luteinizing hormone
Melatonin
Mineralocorticoids
Ovaries
Oxytocin
Phlebotomist
Pineal gland
Pituitary gland

Plasma
Posterior pituitary lobe
Progesterone
Prolactin
Secondary sex characteristics
Serum
Sex hormones
Target cells
Target organs
Testes
Testosterone
Thyrotropic hormone
Vasopressin
Venipuncture

Chapter Five: Facial Musculature

Most people probably don't know it, but the word *muscle* actually comes from the Latin word for "little mouse"; this is because it was thought that flexing muscles looked like little mice scurrying around under the skin. In fact, nearly everything you do involves your muscles in some way. Even when you sleep, your heart muscles keep blood pumping throughout your body, your respiratory muscles keep your lungs moving, and the muscles controlling your eyes keep your eyeballs in relatively constant motion. Indeed, *all bodily movement* is dependent on muscular activity.

This includes the muscles you use to make various facial expressions. When you smile at a friend, frown at an enemy, grit your teeth in frustration, or raise your eyebrows in surprise, it is your facial muscles that make these movements possible. In this chapter, we will discuss the structure and function of the muscular system, in general, and of the facial musculature, in particular. We will then explore some of the methods by which researchers can measure facial muscle activity, using both physiological and observational approaches. Finally, we will discuss research on the facial expression of emotion, which is perhaps the principal application of muscle measurement techniques in the field of human communication.

Structure and Function of Facial Musculature

You have over 650 individual muscles in your body, but you can divide all muscle tissues into one of three types: **skeletal muscles**, **smooth**

muscles, and **cardiac muscles**. As you might guess, skeletal muscles are generally attached to bones, although some facial muscles are attached to skin tissues instead. Skeletal muscles are responsible for your ability to perform almost every voluntary movement, from waving to running to smiling. When your brain sends the command "pick up my pencil" to your arm and hand, it is the skeletal muscles that respond by contracting to move your hand to where your pencil is sitting and to move your fingers to grasp it.

Skeletal muscles are the only type of muscles under our voluntary control. However, that doesn't mean that all skeletal muscle movements are voluntary. Skeletal muscles also make your reflex actions possible. If you accidentally touch something hot, for example, the skeletal muscles in your arm and shoulder immediately contract to pull your hand away. This happens automatically, even though you have not consciously willed it to happen.

Skeletal muscles are sometimes referred to as **striated muscles** because the fibers of skeletal muscles look like they are covered with stripes. When viewed under a microscope, some of these strips appear darker than others; the darker stripes are sometimes called *A-bands* and the lighter ones are called *I-bands.* Most skeletal muscles are attached to bones through strong, non-elastic fibers known as **tendons**. Strain or overuse of particular muscles, particularly in middle-aged adults, can cause a painful inflammation of the tendons, a condition known as **tendonitis**.

Smooth muscles are found primarily in the walls of hollow organs, such as the stomach, bladder, respiratory passages, and bowels. The muscles of the blood vessels are also smooth muscles. Unlike skeletal muscles, we do not normally exercise any conscious control over smooth muscle movement. That is, we don't need to "tell" our stomachs to digest food or our blood vessels to pump blood – rather, these things happen automatically to keep the body functioning properly. As their name implies, smooth muscles don't have the stripes that characterize skeletal muscles. Instead, their appearance is more uniform; they may be thought of as *unstriated* muscles.

Finally, cardiac muscles are found only on the walls of the heart. Their job is to make the heart contract, or beat, in order to pump blood throughout the body. They share some similarities with both skeletal and smooth muscles. Cardiac muscles are striated, like skeletal muscles; however, they act involuntarily, without conscious control, like smooth muscles. The heart's internal pacemaker regulates the rhythm with which the cardiac muscles contract to make the heart beat.

Your face has a number of different muscles, some of which function primarily for chewing and others of which allow you to form facial expressions. The ability to make facial expressions is uniquely human, and the human face is capable of making a wide variety of expressions, many of which are related to the communication of emotion. Although a number of muscles are involved even in a simple smile, we will focus here on those facial muscles that are the most important in the formation of facial expressions. These include the **frontalis**, the **procerus**, the **orbicularis oculi**, the **orbicularis oris**, the **zygomaticus major**, and the **corrugator supercilii**.

The frontalis is the largest of the facial muscles. It covers the frontal bone of the skull, underlying your forehead. The frontalis is the muscle used to raise your eyebrows and wrinkle your forehead, which typically indicate that you are surprised or interested in something. Contrariwise, the procerus is a small muscle located above your nose, right between your eyebrows. It pulls your eyebrows downward when you express anger.

The orbicularis oculi is one of two facial muscles that is not connected to any skeletal bone, but only to the facial tissue. It circles the eye. The orbicularis oculi has two parts, an outer and an inner part. The outer part forces the eye shut, such as when you squint; the inner part closes your eye gently, such as when you blink. The orbicularis oculi is also responsible for the wrinkles, or "crow's feet," that you get on the sides of your eyes when you smile.

The other facial muscle that is not connected to bone is the orbicularis oris, which circles the lips. It is sometimes referred to as the *kissing muscle*, because it gives you the ability to pucker your lips to kiss or to say the word "who."

The zygomaticus major runs diagonally on either side of your face, from just in front of your ear to the corner of your mouth. It is sometimes called the *smile muscle*, because it allows you to pull the corners of your mouth upward to form a smile. Most positive facial expressions – from pleasantness to ecstatic joy – involve the zygomaticus major. Finally, the corrugator supercilii lies just above the orbicularis oculi over each eye. It pulls your eyebrows toward each other, creating the vertical wrinkles, or furrows, in between your eyes. This is often seen in facial expressions of concern or worry. In fact, most negative facial expressions – from minor irritation to outright agony – involve the corrugator supercilii. This muscle is also known as **Coiter's muscle**.

These are not the only muscles of the face, to be certain, but they are among the most important when it comes to forming facial expressions. How is it that researchers can study the movement of various facial muscles, however? In the next section, we will discuss three types of measurement strategies that communication scientists can use.

Measuring Facial Muscle Activity

Researchers who are interested in knowing more about facial expressions and the functions they serve in communication often need to measure the activities of facial muscles in some way. In this section, we will discuss three approaches to the measurement of facial musculature. The first, involving a technique called **electromyography**, captures the electrical signals generated by muscles as they contract. The second involves observational coding of specific muscle movements, an approach we will refer to as **micro-coding**. The third approach also involves observational coding, but of expressions rather than specific muscle movements; we will refer to this as **macro-coding**.

Electromyography

Like other parts of your body, your muscles generate small electrical signals whenever they contract. The technique of electromyography

(**EMG**) is designed to record this electrical activity as a way of assessing when – and to what degree – various muscles contract. The EMG can capture electrical signals from muscles in one of two ways. The most common approach in research settings is to use electrodes that are placed on the surface of the skin, directly over the specific muscle or muscle group that is being investigated. In facial EMG, for instance, electrodes might be placed on the forehead to record the activity of the frontalis, and on the cheeks to capture signals from the zygomaticus major. By contrast, clinical work with EMG often uses very thin needle-electrodes that are inserted directly into the muscle tissue to capture the electrical signal. Although this is clearly a more invasive approach, it tends to generate more accurate results because the signals are being recorded directly from within the muscles.

EMG can be used to record the activity of pretty much any muscles in the body. Our discussion here will focus on facial EMG in particular, however, since the facial muscles are so important to the ways that people communicate. Although EMG is usually administered in a clinical or laboratory setting, some researchers have refined the technique of using an ambulatory EMG, which allows for the recording of muscular activity for up to 18 hours a day.

Like the electroencephalogram (EEG), which we discussed in Chapter Two, the EMG produces results in a waveform, which are either plotted on a scrolling paper or are represented on a computer screen. The wave indicates the levels of microvolts (μV) being produced by the muscles under investigation. The EMG waveform has high frequency and relatively erratic amplitude, because muscles vary in the frequency and intensity with which they contract. Thus, the EMG waveform does not typically show the rhythmic pattern of, say, a heart rate wave.

As we will discuss in greater detail below, a typical use of EMG in communication research is in the study of how people react to various visual stimuli, including facial expressions of emotion.

Micro-Coding Approaches

A second, and very different, approach to studying the activities of the facial muscles is to use an observational coding system. Several systems have been developed for this purpose, including the Maximally Discriminative Facial Movement Coding System (MAX: Izard, 1979), the Facial Affect Scoring Technique (FAST: Ekman, Friesen, & Tomkins, 1972), and A System for Identifying Affect Expressions by Holistic Judgment (AFFEX: Izard, Dougherty, & Hembree, 1983). Perhaps the most comprehensive is the **Facial Action Coding System** (FACS), developed by Ekman and Friesen (1978). FACS is a system whereby trained coders (usually viewing videotaped facial behavior in slow motion) can manually code all facial displays that are possible for humans to make, based on various combinations of their facial muscle movement. FACS coders look for 33 *action units* (AUs), each of which is comprised of one or more muscle contractions. For instance, one AU is used to describe the tightening of the lips, done through contraction of the orbicularis oris. Another is used to code the wink, which involves movement of the orbicularis oculi.

An important aspect of FACS is that it only codes for specific facial movements; it does not code for emotion displays. In other words, FACS would code a smile simply as a contraction of the zygomaticus major muscle; it does not code the movement as a sign of happiness. The connection between the facial muscle movement and the emotional display is outside the scope of the coding system, making FACS a purely descriptive approach. This is what we mean when we refer to FACS as a micro-coding system.

As you might imagine, it takes a great deal of time to learn how to code behavior using FACS. Coders complete an extensive training program and must pass a certification test that requires them to code videotapes of spontaneous facial expressions with a high degree of reliability. Even after coders have achieved certification, it still takes a long time to code facial behavior using FACS. In a typical study, facial behaviors are coded from videotapes using a stop-frame method, whereby every frame of videotape (1/25th or 1/30th of a second, for instance) is examined and coded separately. This is an important feature of FACS, given that facial expressions can often be extremely short in duration. However, it requires an enormous amount of time and effort to code even the shortest of interactions. Research on FACS indicates that it does produce reliable coding, however (Sayette, Cohn, Wertz, Perrott, & Parrott, 2001), and FACS has been used in research on a wide variety of topics.

Macro-Coding Approaches

As we've mentioned, one limitation of EMG and micro-coding as options for studying facial behavior is that they only take account of which muscles are contracting. It is then left to the researcher, or to students or other consumers of the research, to infer what those movements *mean* as communication signals. Contraction of the zygomaticus major, which results in a smile, might mean that the subject is happy; on the other hand, it might mean that he or she is smiling out of frustration, or disappointment, or wicked satisfaction. In other words, it is difficult – if not impossible – to "map" emotions directly onto facial muscular activity. The same facial expression might suggest more than one emotion, and two people experiencing the same emotion might convey it using different expressions.

A third option for researchers interested in studying facial muscular activity is to code muscle movements for the types of emotions they convey. That is, instead of recording (either electronically or via human coding) which muscles in the face contract at which times, this approach records which emotions, or affects, are being displayed by the configuration of muscle movement observed in the face at any given moment. We thus refer to this approach as *macro-coding*.

If there isn't perfect correspondence between muscular movements and emotions, though, how can researchers code which emotion is being displayed just by looking at the face? That is, how can we do macro-coding? Importantly, this approach relies on culturally specific knowledge about facial emotion displays. Any researcher who is properly trained can operate an EMG or engage in micro-coding of specific muscle movements – but when it comes to inferring what those movements mean, cultural knowledge becomes important. Not all cultures display emotions in quite the same way, nor to the same intensity. If you've traveled much in various parts of the world, you know what we mean. Americans tend to be fairly expressive, especially of positive emotions, which is obvious anytime you watch a sporting event or game show on television. By contrast, people from other cultures, such as the Japanese, are brought up to control their emotion displays more tightly, so good news or good fortune do not typically bring the same outburst of joy to the face of a Japanese person as they do to the typical American.

If you're unaware of these types of differences, then it would be difficult to do macro-coding on people from cultures different than your own. You might look at the stoic face of a Japanese college student and conclude that he or she is not as happy as the American who is jumping up and down, screaming, and hugging everyone in sight – yet, this may not be a valid conclusion. Culturally specific knowledge is, therefore, an important part of the macro-coding approach.

In the social sciences, perhaps the best-known system for doing macro-coding of facial expressions is the **Specific Affect Coding System** (**SPAFF**) developed by John Gottman and colleagues. In this system (which can also be applied to vocal cues, rather than facial expressions), coders are trained in how to spot a number of specific emotions when observing facial expressions (the exact number of different emotions depends on the version of SPAFF being used). For instance, as a SPAFF coder, you would be trained in how to recognize not only primary emotions, such as joy, anger, fear, or surprise, but also more complex emotions, such as shame, suspicion, or envy. SPAFF coding is typically done by watching a participant (via videotape) and coding which of several specific emotions the participant is conveying with his or her facial expression at each window of time (e.g., every five seconds, every two minutes). In addition to identifying the emotion being displayed, coders sometimes also rate the display for its intensity – to distinguish, for instance, between mild happiness and downright ecstasy.

SPAFF has been extensively tested for its validity as a coding system and has been used in a number of important long-term studies, usually with romantic couples. We will discuss some of the applications of SPAFF in the following section.

Of course, FACS and SPAFF are not the only micro- and macro-coding options available, but they are among the best validated and most commonly used examples of each type of system, which is why we highlight them here. In the next section, we will discuss some of the ways that EMG, FACS, and SPAFF have been used in research on facial emotion displays. Certainly, facial muscles serve purposes other than to convey emotion, but there is general consensus among nonverbal communication researchers that the expression of emotion is one of the most – if not, *the* most – important communicative functions of the face. We confine our discussion accordingly, for this reason.

Applications with Facial Emotion Displays

All three methods of quantifying facial musculature – electromyography, micro coding, and macro coding – can be used to study how people express various types of emotions on their faces. This is important because the face is the primary site of emotion displays in humans (Knapp, 1978). As a result, looking at the ways in which people use their faces to convey various emotions can teach us much about how humans communicate.

In one study, Herrera, Bourgeois, and Hess (1998) used EMG to study people's patterns for responding to facial displays of emotion with similar displays. You probably already know that when people see a particular facial display of emotion (e.g., a happy face, an angry face), they often mimic that expression on their own faces as a way of communicating empathy with the other person. (When a friend tells you of her relationship troubles and expresses her sadness on her face, you typically express sadness on your own face in response, so that your friend knows you are empathizing with her.) Researchers call this type of behavior *facial mimicry*, and Herrera and colleagues were interested to see whether people do this more when talking with someone of the same ethnicity than when talking with someone who has a different ethnic background. They predicted that most people use facial mimicry more when their conversational partners are of the same ethnicity than when they are from a different ethnic group.

To test this idea, the researchers recruited two ethnic groups – French Canadians and Asians – to take part in their experiment. Each participant had sensors from an EMG placed on or near the orbicularis oculi, the zygomaticus major, and the corrugator supercilii. Then, each participant was shown a series of photographs of either Caucasian or Asian faces expressing happiness, sadness, anger, or fear, and the researchers looked to see how each participant's own facial expression would change in response to the photos. Their predictions were confirmed – both groups showed little facial mimicry when looking at an emotion display made by a member of the opposite ethnic group, and more facial mimicry when the display was from someone in their own ethnic group. More interestingly, those participants who had negative feelings about the other ethnic group actually showed *counter-mimicry* when looking at facial expressions from the other group – that is, they smiled at expressions of sadness or made angry faces at expressions of happiness.

While the Herrera et al. study looked at facial emotion displays within the context of ethnicity, other research has focused on how people's communication of emotions affects, and is affected by, the quality of their relationships. In one such study, Gottman, Levenson, and Woodin (2001) had 79 married couples take part in a laboratory study in which they were first interviewed about the history of their marriage and were then made to engage in an interaction in which they discussed the events of the day, a mutually identified source of conflict in their marriage, and a mutually identified pleasant topic. During the interaction, the researchers took measures of heart rate and galvanic skin response from the participants (along with some other physiological measures). Afterward, the videotapes of the husbands and wives in each interaction were coded using a version of FACS specifically designed for coding emotions (called the EMFACS). Finally, 73 of the couples were contacted four years later and were asked to report on the status of their marriage (how satisfying it was, whether the husband and/or wife had seriously considered divorce, etc.).

The researchers found a number of important patterns. During the laboratory interaction, the more the wife in each couple felt "flooded" or overwhelmed by her husband's complaints about the marriage, the more her husband expressed contempt on his face and the less often both spouses smiled genuinely. When husbands believed that their marital problems were too significant to work out, they showed more anger and insincere smiles on their faces and their wives showed more sadness. The more the wives felt this way about their problems, the more they expressed disgust on their faces and the more their husbands expressed contempt.

Importantly, however, husbands' and wives' facial expressions were not simply related to how they felt at the time they were interacting. You'll recall that most couples were contacted four years later to find out the status of their marriage at that time. During this follow-up, each couple was asked to report how many months in the previous four years that they had spent separated from each other (if at all). The number of months couples had been separated was predicted by how much the husband expressed fear and insincere smiling and by how much the wife expressed disgust and insincere smiling *during one laboratory conversation four years earlier.* Findings of this nature demonstrate that the emotions we express with our facial muscles are not just associated with what is happening to us at the time, but actually can predict how we will deal with some situations in the future – husbands whose faces expressed a lot of fear during their laboratory conversations spent more time separated from their wives than did husbands whose faces expressed less fear, for instance. Of course, one could make the argument that it was the underlying fear itself – and not really the facial expression of it – that contributed to increased separation time. However, to the extent that our emotions are reflected in the way we communicate with our faces, this distinction between the experience and the expression of the emotion becomes less compelling.

Key Terms

Cardiac muscles
Coiter's muscle
Corrugator supercilii
Electromyography
EMG
Facial Action Coding System
Frontalis
Macro-coding
Micro-coding
Orbicularis oculi
Orbicularis oris
Procerus
Skeletal muscles
Smooth muscles
Specific Affect Coding System
Striated muscles
Tendonitis
Tendons
Zygomaticus major

Chapter Six: Love and Sex

In the first five chapters of this book, we have covered basic anatomy dealing with the brain, the nervous system, the endocrine system, and the muscular system. In the second half of the book, we will be applying your knowledge in these areas by reviewing studies that have looked at various communicative issues from a biological perspective. Each of the next six chapters covers a particular topic and consists of summaries of some empirical studies in that area.

We begin with research on love and sex. Two of the studies reviewed in this chapter deal with the role played by testosterone in the human sexual response. The study by Dabbs investigates the extent to which testosterone influences how much pupil dilation people experience when they hear sexually oriented sounds. Likewise, the study by Carmichael et al. looked at the role played by oxytocin in the sexual response system.

Roney and colleagues investigated how men's testosterone levels change when they interact with women. Finally, McIntyre et al. found that the testosterone levels of men in relationships are moderated by the men's interest in having sex outside the relationship.

Pupil Response Increases During Auditory Sexual Stimuli

Dabbs, J. M. (1997). Testosterone and pupillary response to auditory sexual stimuli. *Physiology & Behavior, 62*, 909-912.

Preview

Subjects categorized as having low, medium, and high levels of testosterone listened to four 30-second recorded stimuli while a computer system measured pupil size. The stimuli dealt with sex, aggression, and two neutral topics. The pupils of both male and female participants dilated more to sexual stimuli than to the other topics. Pupil dilation did not last as long in response to the sexual stimulus for low-testosterone men as for those in other groups.

Description of Study

Testosterone has been related to criminal violence, delinquency, marital discord, and dominance in face-to-face encounters. In cognitive studies, testosterone has been positively related to spatial skill and negatively related to verbal abilities. These findings demonstrate the link between testosterone and long-term behavior and abilities. However, testosterone also can influence behavior in the short term.

Testosterone levels increase before an important contest and continue to increase in the winners, both during and after the contest. Testosterone also predicts sexual activity. Furthermore, it increases in both men and women during sexual activity. Testosterone may increase success in sexual encounters and athletic contests, but the details of how this happens are unknown to researchers. Consequently, there is a further need for studies that attempt to understand how testosterone affects both cognitive and behavioral processes.

Testosterone levels change slower than many other physiological markers that can affect social interaction. While heart rate and blood pressure can change quite quickly, there is a lag of approximately 20 minutes between the signals that the brain sends to increase testosterone and the actual increase itself. Although changes in testosterone happen quite slowly, baseline levels of testosterone might prime individuals to respond differently to the same stimuli.

The present study explored the possibility that individuals with high testosterone are more responsive to sexual and aggressive stimuli than other individuals. Responsiveness was measured by monitoring pupil dilation while subjects listened to sexual, aggressive, and neutral stimuli. The specific question addressed in this study was:

1. How do baseline testosterone levels influence responsiveness to sexual and aggressive stimuli?

Method

The study tested testosterone levels in 66 men and 58 women. Each subject provided a saliva sample that was assayed to obtain baseline testosterone levels. Pupil size and pupil responsiveness were measured using a computer controlled infrared pupillometry system. Specifically, the ISCAN pupillometer illuminates the eye with infrared light, records a video image of the eye, and the computer detects the edge of the pupils to measure their size.

While participants' pupil size and pupil responsiveness were being measured, participants listened to four audiotaped stimuli, each lasting 30 seconds with 10 seconds of silence in between. Subjects listened to sexual, aggressive, and two neutral stimuli. The aggressive stimulus was a heated argument between a girlfriend and boyfriend about unfaithfulness. The sexual stimulus was a vocal and noisy episode of sexual intercourse between a boyfriend and girlfriend. One control stimulus was a conversation between two old cowboys from the movie *Lonesome Dove,* and the other was an airline hostess greeting passengers at the beginning of a long flight. The stimuli were given to participants in one of four counterbalanced orders.

Results

General results indicated that pupils dilated about 3% when participants listened to the talk, airline, and fight stimuli and about 6% when they listened to the sexual stimulus. After dividing participants into three groups based on their baseline testosterone levels, results indicated that, across stimuli, there was more pupil dilation among high-testosterone subjects.

Responses to the three nonsexual stimuli appeared to be similar to one another. Furthermore, each of the three nonsexual stimuli appeared to be different from the sexual stimulus. Specifically, pupil dilation was larger and lasted longer during the sexual stimulus compared to the nonsexual stimuli. Moreover, there were different reactions over time between the nonsexual and the sexual stimuli.

When participants heard nonsexual stimuli, pupil dilation increased for about five seconds and then decreased slowly to below average levels for both sexes. When participants heard the sexual stimulus, pupil dilation was greater than the nonsexual stimuli, but it also lasted longer, about 15 seconds. While most participants showed a slow decrease in pupil size after 15 seconds, in low-testosterone males, pupil size decreased rapidly after 15 seconds.

Key Ideas

- Testosterone has been related to criminal violence, delinquency, marital discord, and dominance in face-to-face encounters.

- Across stimuli, there was more pupil dilation among high-testosterone subjects.

- Pupil dilation was larger and lasted longer during the sexual stimulus compared to the other three nonsexual stimuli.

OXYTOCIN LEVELS INCREASE DURING AND AFTER SEXUAL STIMULATION

Carmichael, M. S., Humbert R., Dixen, J., Palmisano, G., Greenleaf, W., & Davidson, J. M. (1987). Plasma oxytocin increases in the human sexual response. *Journal of Clinical Endocrinology and Metabolism, 64*, 27-31.

Preview

The purpose of this study was to determine whether or not oxytocin levels change during and after human sexual activity and to understand the pattern of that change. In this study oxytocin levels were measured before, during, and after private sexual self-stimulation to orgasm in both men and women. Results indicated that oxytocin levels increased during sexual arousal in both men and women. Moreover, oxytocin levels were significantly higher during orgasm than before the start of sexual stimulation.

Description of Study

Few studies have examined the relationship between sexual arousal and orgasm and the release of hormones in the body. Specifically, little attention has been given the possible role that oxytocin plays in the human sexual response. In women, oxytocin is best known for facilitating milk ejection during breast-feeding and enhancing uterine contractions during childbirth. In addition, oxytocin is known for increasing maternal behavior and facilitating pair bonding. Consequently, the role of oxytocin in the human sexual response, for both men and women, needs further study.

Researchers argue that oxytocin levels increase during sexual interaction to cause smooth muscle contractions, which in turn increase the likelihood of reproductive success. Consequently, this study provides a detailed analysis of the release of oxytocin in both men and women before, during, and after sexual activity and orgasm. The specific question addressed in this study was:

1. How do oxytocin levels change in both men and women before, during, and after sexual activity and orgasm?

Method

The study tested oxytocin levels in 13 women and nine men before, during, and after sexual activity and orgasm. Each subject participated in two sessions with a four to five week delay between testing.

Oxytocin levels were obtained from blood samples. Samples were taken at either two or one minute intervals from six minutes before the start of sexual self-stimulation through five minutes after orgasm. Oxytocin levels were measured by radioimmunoassay.

Results

Oxytocin levels in both men and women who only had one orgasm increased significantly from the baseline measurement to orgasm. Oxytocin levels in women who had more than one orgasm rose from the baseline measurement to the first orgasm and continued to increase through the second orgasm. Furthermore, in women who had more than one orgasm, oxytocin levels remained elevated five minutes after orgasm. Mean oxytocin levels during self-stimulation were higher for women than for men. Likewise, the mean oxytocin levels during orgasm were higher for women than men. There was no relationship between the duration of self-stimulation and oxytocin levels. Baseline oxytocin levels were greater for women in the luteal phase of the menstrual cycle compared to those in the follicular phase. However, there were no significant differences in oxytocin levels during orgasm between women in these different phases of the menstrual cycle.

Key Ideas

- In women, increased oxytocin causes smooth muscle contractions, which facilitates reproductive success.
- Levels of oxytocin increased after sexual stimulation and orgasm in both men and women.
- Women have greater oxytocin levels than men both before and after orgasm.

MEN'S TESTOSTERONE IN A ROMANTIC RELATIONSHIP IS MODERATED BY EXTRAPAIR SEXUAL INTEREST

McIntyre, M., Gangestad, S. W., Gray, P. B., Chapman, J. F., Burnham, T. C., O'Rourke, M. T., & Thornhill, R. (2006). Romantic involvement often reduces men's testosterone levels – but not always: The moderating role of extrapair sexual interest. *Journal of Personality and Social Psychology, 91*, 642-651.

Preview

Men's testosterone levels appear to be affected by their level of romantic involvement. It is believed that, as mating effort (the investment of time into both same-sex competition and seeking a mate) for men increases, testosterone levels also increase to help fuel the mating drive. Conversely, men who are in a relationship show lower testosterone levels than single men, signaling the lack of effort being put into winning a mate. This study finds that testosterone are significantly affected by both current and alternative relationships.

Description of Study

A large body of research examines effects of the steroid hormone testosterone on mating effort. Testosterone promotes bone and muscle growth and appears to fuel the competitive and sexual drives. For example, one recent study found that men's testosterone increased when they interacted with a woman (and even more so when the woman thought they were attempting to impress her). This study examined whether married men showed lower levels of testosterone than unmarried men. Additionally, the researchers questioned whether men in committed relationships showed lower levels of testosterone than single men, and whether divorced men's testosterone dropped when they remarried. The researchers believed that these decreases in testosterone are due to the lack of mating effort done by the individual in a committed relationship/marriage (not searching for a romantic partner), reducing their need for the hormone.

Essentially, if a man is more open to the idea of being unfaithful in a relationship, he would still put time and energy into the mating effort, whereas a man who is only interested in remaining faithful to the relationship would put limited resources into the mating effort. The specific prediction of the two studies was:

1. In men, the amount of extra-pair sexual interest moderates the association between romantic relationship status and testosterone.

Method

Study 1 used 102 college students to investigate extra-pair sexual interest with the Sociosexual Orientation Inventory (SOI), measuring whether individuals have a restricted sociosexual orientation (sex only within the relationship) or an unrestricted sociosexual orientation (sex outside the relationship). Researchers proposed that the score of the SOI would moderate the relationship between relationship status and testosterone. A saliva sample was also taken by the participants and analyzed by the researchers in order to measure testosterone. The researchers then split their sample into three groups: 37 were currently in a relationship; 44 were single but reported being in a relationship during the past three years; and, 21 were single and had not been in a relationship during the past three years.

Study 2 involved 69 heterosexual college-aged men. The participants were required to come to two lab sessions. In the first, the participant filled out a questionnaire, which included demographic information, the SOI, and the question, "Would you ever consider having an affair (sex with a person other than a main, current relationship partner) behind the back of your relationship partner?" For the final question, participants could only choose an option saying that they would never consider it, or an option saying that they could imagine that situation presenting itself. In addition, participants detailed their history of extra-pair sex. Finally, they were presented with a test tube and instructed to take a saliva sample upon awakening the next morning, thus controlling for diurnal variation in testosterone. The second lab session consisted of the participants bringing in their saliva sample and being debriefed while the researchers analyzed the saliva sample for testosterone.

Results

In Study 1, testosterone level for individuals in a relationship was moderated by the individuals' interest in an extra-pair sexual relationship. Individuals in a relationship showed a smaller decrement in testosterone levels (compared to single individuals) when they reported a higher interest in an extra-pair sexual relationship. Furthermore, individuals with more relationship experience had higher testosterone levels than their less experienced counterparts. When the researchers analyzed the group of participants currently in a relationship by themselves, they discovered a significant positive relationship between the SOI and testosterone when controlling for the length of the relationship. However, as predicted, SOI did not significantly predict levels of testosterone for either group of single men, supporting the conclusion that relationship status affects testosterone, though not supportive of the conclusion that testosterone helps push men toward romantic relationships. Therefore, the hypothesis was mostly supported.

In Study 2, all three of the extra-pair sex variables were significantly correlated with each other. Thus, all variables were combined and treated as a single variable of extra-pair interest. As in earlier studies, single men had significantly higher testosterone levels than men in relationships. Further, the extra-pair sexual interest score significantly interacted with relationship status, as the decrease in testosterone for individuals in a relationship was moderated by the amount of extra-pair sexual interest. The researchers also split up the sample of men in relationships into three groups: those who were married/ engaged, those who were living with their partner, and those who were simply dating. Within those groups as well, extra-pair sexual interest significantly predicted levels of testosterone, moderating the impact of the individuals remaining in a committed relationship.

Key Ideas

- Male interest in sex outside of the relationship moderates the level of testosterone while currently in a relationship.
- Testosterone levels are higher for single men than for men in a relationship.
- The act of sexual selection (or mating effort) is an adaptive behavior that increases men's capacity for competition with the same sex and seeking a mate.

MEN'S TESTOSTERONE INCREASES WHEN THEY ATTEMPT TO IMPRESS WOMEN

Roney, J. R., Mahler, S. V., & Maestripieri, D. (2003). Behavioral and hormonal responses of men to brief interactions with women. *Evolution and Human Behavior, 24*, 365-375.

Preview

Previous research indicates several physiological and behavioral reactions from men during conversations with potential mating partners. The current study examined increases in the levels of the hormone testosterone, along with a battery of psychological measures during male communication with both male and female partners. When men communicated with women, they experienced a significant rise in testosterone, and this was especially true when the woman believed that the man was attempting to impress her. The researchers linked these findings to various evolutionary patterns.

Description of Study

Across the vertebrate animal kingdom, males experience a physiological response to communication with potential mating partners. This is referred to as a *mating response*, defined as a significant increase in certain sexual hormones brought on by courtship or sexual behavior. However, little research has examined whether the mating response also occurs in men, although a few studies have found heightened testosterone levels in men after watching a sexually explicit movie.

This study sought to ascertain whether men would experience a rise in testosterone as a result of interacting with attractive women. Men interacting with women were compared to men interacting with other men. If testosterone is related to mating effort, then it should rise only as a result of interaction with women (assuming the men are heterosexual). The specific prediction of the study was:

1. Male courtship behavior directed toward a female partner increases male testosterone level.

Method

Researchers recruited 39 heterosexual male participants, who were randomly assigned to have a brief conversation with either one of two potential male partners or one of five potential female partners. Upon entering the lab, participants were asked to complete a consent form and then gave a saliva sample to measure baseline levels of testosterone. After five minutes, the confederates entered the room, while the researcher (using a predetermined excuse) left. This left the participant and confederate alone in the room for approximately five minutes. The confederate was instructed to engage in friendly conversation with the participant, making the participant comfortable and encouraging normal interaction. When the researcher returned, the participant completed a questionnaire while the confederate completed a form detailing his or her perception of the participant and the interaction. A final saliva sample was then collected from the participant (roughly 15 minutes after the interaction). At that time, the participant was informed of the purpose of the study and asked to fill out a form detailing his perception of the confederate (including physical attractiveness, potential as a mating partner, and enjoyment of the interaction).

Results

As predicted, testosterone levels in men rose significantly after their interaction with the female confederates, whereas there was no significant rise after the interaction with the male confederates. Testosterone levels rose even more when males rated the female confederates as more attractive and the female confederates rated the male participant as trying to impress them. Consequently, testosterone levels rose even more when males were actively engaged in the mating effort.

The researchers suggested several interesting conclusions from these results. First, the findings lend support to the claim that testosterone increases for men after engaging in interactions with women. Hormones also appear to play a significant role in human sexual arousal, moderating certain behavioral tactics (especially seeking to impress) in interactions with individuals of the opposite sex. Perhaps the most interesting finding of the study was that the level of testosterone was highest in men when the female confederate perceived that the man was attempting to impress her. Thus, there appears to be a link between testosterone and certain human courting behaviors. While no causal relationship can currently be postulated, there exists a clear correlation between human courtship behavior and testosterone.

Key Ideas

- Men's testosterone levels rose after the men interacted with a woman.
- Testosterone levels were highest when the woman perceived that the man was attempting to impress her.
- There appears to exist a link between human courtship and the hormone testosterone.

Chapter Seven: Stress

The research summarized in this chapter deals with how people handle stress. The first paper, by Kirschbaum and colleagues, investigates the extent to which healthy adult men experience cortisol increases in response to repeated psychological stress.

This is followed by a study by Light et al., in which the researchers looked at the benefits that oxytocin has in terms of lowering blood pressure and reducing stress symptoms. Similarly, Heinrichs and colleagues looked at the ability of social support to increase oxytocin and inhibit the production of cortisol.

Finally, the paper by Roberts and colleagues investigates patterns of cortisol secretion among students engaged in public speaking, a common stressor among undergraduate students.

Cortisol Levels Respond to Repeated Psychological Stress

Kirschbaum, C., Prussner, J. C., Stone, A. A., Federenko, I., Gaab, J., Lintz, D., Schommer, N., & Hellhammer, D. H. (1995). Persistent high cortisol responses to repeated psychological stress in a subpopulation of healthy men. *Psychosomatic Medicine, 57*, 468-474.

Preview

In humans, exposure to stressful situations and events typically results in an increase in cortisol levels. In this study, participants were exposed to psychosocial stressors over the span of five days, with one stress session per day. Analysis revealed that two general stress responses existed in participants. In the *low responder* group, cortisol levels were elevated on the first day. In the *high responder* group, cortisol levels were generally elevated for each of the five experimental treatments. Further analysis revealed that five personality traits could differentiate between the high and low responders.

Description of Study

In humans exposure to stressful situations and events typically results in an increase in cortisol levels. Many times, repeated exposure to the same stressful situations results in a leveling off the cortisol effect over time. For instance, it has been found that military recruits who were followed during parachute training showed a substantial increase in their cortisol level after the first jump. However, repeated jumps did not produce an increase in cortisol levels. Conversely, other studies demonstrate that in rodents repeated stress stimulation can continue to produce significant increases in cortisol levels.

In humans, responsiveness to stressors has been shown to be related to the onset of cardiovascular diseases and other health problems. Responsiveness to acute stress has been implicated as a contributing factor to diseases such as coronary heart disease and hypertension. However, the specific relationship between cortisol responsiveness and disease risks in people has not been investigated.

This study first sought to differentiate between high and low cortisol responders in health adults and then to determine if there were physical and psychological difference between these two groups. The specific questions addressed in this study were:

1. In healthy adults, can high and low cortisol responders be differentiated?
2. Does high versus low responsiveness occur only in initial stress stimulation or does it persist throughout multiple stress exposures?
3. Are there specific personality traits that can differentiate between high and low cortisol responses?

Method

The study consisted of a five-day experiment in which 20 male nonsmokers participated. Each participant was subject to the Trier Social Stress Test (TSST) once a day for five days. The TSST consisted of a public speaking task for five minutes and a mental arithmetic task for five minutes. Each test was in front an audience. Specifically, the participants received a three-minute introduction to the tasks, a ten-minute anticipation/preparation period, and then the ten-minute stress exposure.

Salivary cortisol measures were taken at identical times for all participants for all five days. The saliva samples were taken before receiving the introduction information, after the preparation of the talk, after the public speaking and mental arithmetic, and three posttest samples taken at ten-minute intervals.

After finishing the stress inducing tasks, participants rested before filling out a number of different personality scales to access if there were any connections between personality characteristics and high/low cortisol responsiveness. Specifically, the personality scales measured extraversion, neuroticism, social resonance, dominance, order, prevailing mood, trustfulness, sociability, self-concept of competence, internal control, powerful others control, and chance control. Moreover, a list of general physical health symptoms was used to asses the general heath and well being of participants.

Results

For the total group, saliva cortisol levels rose significantly on all five days. However, cortisol increases were greater on day one than on the following four days. For the total group, analysis revealed an inverse relationship between cortisol response and self-concept (as cortisol response increases, self-concept decreases), social resonance, and trustfulness.

Analysis also revealed that participants could be clustered into two groups based on their mean cortisol responses. This analysis resulted in a high cortisol response group and a low cortisol response group. Further results indicated that high responders showed a large increase over baseline levels in responses to the stress treatments on all five days. However, low responders showed a smaller increase in cortisol level on the first day as compared to the high responders and no significant cortisol increases were found on the following four days.

The authors attempted to find a set of psychological variables that might identify individuals as being high or low cortisol responders. Analysis revealed that six personality variables, in combination, could be used to discriminate between high and low cortisol responders. Specifically, self-concept of competence, internal control, social resonance, prevailing mood, trustfulness, and physical health symptoms discriminated between high and low cortisol responders. More generally, high cortisol responders view themselves as being less attractive than others (negative self-concept), having less self-esteem, and being in a depressed mood more often than low cortisol responders.

Key Ideas

- In humans, exposure to stressful situations results in an increase in cortisol levels.
- High cortisol responders typically react to repeated stressors with continued cortisol increases.
- Low cortisol responders react less to stressors in general and repeated stressors fail to produce cortisol increases.
- High cortisol responders often have a negative self-concept, less self-esteem, and report being in a depressed mood more often than low cortisol responders.

Oxytocin Lowers Blood Pressure and has Anti-Stress Effects

Light, K. C., Smith, T. E., Johns, J. M., Brownley, K. A., Hofheimer, J. A., & Amico, J. A. (2000). Oxytocin responsivity in mothers of infants: A preliminary study of relationships with blood pressure during laboratory stress and normal ambulatory activity. *Health Psychology, 19,* 560-567.

Preview

In animals oxytocin enhances maternal behaviors and decreases blood pressure and the stress response. The purpose of this study was to understand the relationship between oxytocin, blood pressure, and the stress response in breast-feeding and bottle-feeding mothers. General results indicate that oxytocin has antistress and blood pressure lowering effects in mothers. Those with the greatest oxytocin increases after baby contact were primarily breast-feeding mothers, whereas those whose oxytocin levels decreased after baby contact were primarily bottle-feeding mothers. Furthermore, those with oxytocin increases had lower blood pressure and stress after baby feeding at home than those with oxytocin decreases.

Description of Study

The period after an infant's birth is widely known to be a stressful period for mothers. Some mothers adapt both physiologically and psychological to this stressful time better than others. One specific biological factor than may be related to improved functioning is oxytocin.

Oxytocin is produced in both men and women. However, it is best known for its facilitating milk ejection during breast-feeding and enhancing uterine contractions during childbirth. In addition, oxytocin is known for increasing maternal behavior and facilitating pair bonding. It is argued that one way that oxytocin may help increase maternal behavior is by reducing the stress response. Relevant to the present study, oxytocin is known to reduce blood pressure and the stress response in animals; however, this relationship is less established in humans.

The evidence that links oxytocin to lower blood pressure and the stress response is limited. One study found that mothers reported feeling less anxiety, depression, stress, and guilt after breast-feeding (related to oxytocin) than after bottle-feeding. Moreover, the act of breast-feeding has been related to the suppression of the cortisol response in women. However, the relationship between the release of oxytocin and the reduced stress response has not been directly confirmed. The specific predictions addressed in this study were:

1. Mothers who are higher oxytocin responders demonstrate lower overall blood pressure levels and reduced blood pressure reactivity before, during, and after giving a speech about a recent interpersonal conflict.

2. Recent baby contact enhances oxytocin increases evoked by speech stressors.

Method

Participants were 25 mothers (14 breast-feeding and 11 bottle-feeding) who participated in two laboratory sessions, one with and one without their baby. In the 24-hour period between the first and second session, each mother's blood pressure was monitored using an ambulatory blood pressure monitor.

During each laboratory session participants performed a speech about a stressful experience. Testing was identical for the two laboratory sessions with the only difference being baby contact. On the no-baby-contact day, mothers were instructed not to bring their baby with them for the appointment and to allow a minimum of one hour between participation in the study and their most recent baby feeding. On the baby-contact day, mothers brought their infants with them. During the speech stressor the baby was placed in a carrier or stroller and watched by staff members. After the completion of the speech, the infant was brought back to the mother.

Oxytocin levels were obtained through blood samples taken throughout the speech stressor and during a recovery period afterwards. Oxytocin response in participants was measured by the change in oxytocin levels from the baseline to the speech. Participants were grouped based on whether their oxytocin levels increased or decreased in response to the speech stressor.

Results

The oxytocin increase group included primarily breast-feeding mothers, whereas the oxytocin decrease group included primarily bottle-feeding mothers. Oxytocin increases were larger on the baby-contact day than compared to the no-baby-contact day. Overall, the systolic and diastolic blood pressure levels were higher in the oxytocin decrease group than the oxytocin increase group. Consequently, higher oxytocin responses were associated with lower overall blood pressure on both test days.

In women with oxytocin increases, blood pressure reductions were observed after the speech with baby contact. Mothers who showed decreases in oxytocin to stress had higher diastolic blood pressure and greater diastolic blood pressure reactivity to speech preparation and recovery compared with mothers who had oxytocin increases. All participants, regardless of their oxytocin response showed reduced systolic blood pressure reactivity to the speech stressor after baby contact as compared to the no-baby control condition.

Key Ideas

- Oxytocin enhances maternal behaviors and facilitates pair bonding.

- In humans the release of oxytocin may be related to decreases in blood pressure and the stress response.

- Higher oxytocin responses were associated with lower overall blood pressure.

- Mothers who showed decreases in oxytocin to stress had higher diastolic blood pressure and greater diastolic blood pressure reactivity to speech preparation and recovery compared with mothers who had oxytocin increases.

Social Support and Oxytocin Suppress Responses to Stress

Heinrichs, M., Baumgartner, T., Kirschbaum, C., & Ehlert, U. (2003). Social support and oxytocin interact to suppress cortisol and subjective responses to psychosocial stress. *Biological Psychiatry, 54,* 1389-1398.

Preview

This study was designed to test the effects of social support and oxytocin on cortisol, mood, and anxiety responses during social stress situations. Participants were randomly assigned to receive intranasal oxytocin or a placebo before the social stressor and receive either social support from their best friend during the preparation or receive no social support. Results indicated that cortisol levels were suppressed by social support in response to stress. Most importantly, the combination of oxytocin and social support demonstrated the lowest cortisol response in addition to increased calmness and decreased anxiety during stress.

Description of Study

Evidence exists that lack of social contact and support contributes to psychological and physiological health problems such as depression and coronary heart disease. Conversely, positive social interactions have been shown to be beneficial to health and longevity. Specifically, research has shown that higher reported levels of social support are related to positive effects on cardiovascular reactivity and blood pressure, depression, and schizophrenia. In addition, social support has been related to markers of physiological stress. Specifically, higher levels of social support have been related to lower cortisol levels found in saliva and lower cardiovascular reactivity.

Although much is known about the positive effects of social support with respect to health and risk, little is known about the physiological mechanisms that social support triggers. More specifically, it is unclear how positive social interactions and social support suppress the physiological stress reaction system. For example, it is possible that social support stimulates other regulatory systems that suppress the stress response.

In animal studies, oxytocin has been shown to have both behavioral and physiological stress reducing effects, in addition to promoting positive social interactions. According to research, oxytocin inhibits the stress-inducing activity of the hypothalamic-pituitary-adrenal (HPA) axis. Furthermore, oxytocin has been related to social attachment and prosocial behavior. However, support for oxytocin as an underlying biological mechanism for the reduction of stress and anxiety during positive social interactions in humans has yet to be obtained. The specific question addressed in this study was:

1. What are the effects of oxytocin and social support on mood, anxiety and responses to social stress?

Method

Thirty-seven healthy men participated in the study. All participants underwent a physical evaluation to screen out chronic diseases, mental disorders, medication, smoking, and drug and alcohol abuse. Participants refrained from food and drink (other than water) for two hours prior to the experiment and from exercise, caffeine, and alcohol 24 hours before the experiment.

Two weeks before the experiment, subjects were randomly instructed either to bring a best friend (either male or female) along with them to the experiment (social support condition) or to come alone (no social support condition). Friends were told to be as helpful as possible during the ten-minute preparation time for the speech task and to offer both instrumental and emotional support.

Participants were also randomly assigned to receive intranasally either a single dose of oxytocin or a placebo. Administration of the oxytocin or placebo took place 50 minutes before the stress exposure.

All experimental sessions took place between 2:00 p.m. and 4:00 p.m. to control for diurnal changes in cortisol levels. The experiment lasted approximately two hours. Participants were asked to perform the Trier Social Stress Test (TSST), which consists of a public speaking task and a mental arithmetic task, both performed in front of an audience. Participants were required to give a five-minute mock job interview to an unknown panel followed by a five-minute mental arithmetic exercise performed out loud. Before performing each of these tasks participants were given ten minutes to prepare for these tasks with either support from their friend or by themselves.

Salivary cortisol levels were obtained eight times over the course of the stress session. Specifically, cortisol samples were obtained before the preparation phase (20 minutes before TSST), immediately before the stress (1 minute before TSST), and six samples were collected during the 60-minute post-stress period.

Psychological measures included self-report scales of depression and anxiety. The general availability of social support was obtained by measuring the perceived availability of social support resources available to the participant. Finally, an assessment of mood was utilized. Both mood and state anxiety were assessed before and after the stress exposure.

Results

As expected, the total group of participants (all four conditions) responded to the social stress with increased cortisol levels. There was a significant effect for social support, in that those who received social support had smaller cortisol responses than those who did not. More importantly, there was an interaction effect between social support and oxytocin, with the lowest cortisol concentrations after the stress test found in participants who received both social support and oxytocin.

With respect to mood and anxiety, analysis revealed another interaction between social support and oxytocin on calmness. Participants without social support and with the placebo exhibited a decrease in calmness during stress. In contrast, participants who received either social support or oxytocin or both showed increasing calmness during the stress procedure. Furthermore, there was a trend toward an interaction between social support and oxytocin on state anxiety. Specifically, the group without social support and with the placebo showed an increase in anxiety, whereas participants with social support, oxytocin, or both, showed decreases in anxiety during stress.

Key Ideas

- Lack of social contact and support contributes to psychological and physiological health problems.
- Positive social interactions and social support are shown to be beneficial to health and longevity.
- Social support is associated with a reduced cortisol response.
- Social support and oxytocin interact to reduce cortisol and anxiety responses in men.

SALIVARY CORTISOL IS AN INDICATOR OF STATE ANXIETY IN PUBLIC SPEAKERS

Roberts, J. B., Sawyer, C. R., & Behnke, R. R. (2004). A neurological representation of speech state anxiety: Mapping salivary cortisol levels of public speakers. *Western Journal of Communication*, *68*, 219-231.

Preview

The neuroendocrine hormone cortisol is produced during anxiety inducing activities. The present study examined cortisol levels during situations of state anxiety. Specifically, the study attempted to map cortisol levels of public speakers over time. Results indicate that cortisol levels decrease over time. Moreover, cortisol levels were related to measures of the speakers' state anxiety.

Description of Study

When examining speech state anxiety, most researchers offer explanations of this phenomenon based on the functioning of particular biological mechanisms. This explanation is based on the idea that when we experience fear, particular biological mechanisms get initiated to help us deal with that fear. In the past, research on speech state anxiety has focused on such biological reactions as heart rate and blood pressure.

Although heart rate and blood pressure are often examined in reference to speech state anxiety, these biological indicators are a measure of physiological arousal and are not always indicators of speech state anxiety. Thus, these biological indicators are seen as a secondary indicator as heart rate and blood pressure can increase under emotional states other than anxiety. Consequently, the goal of this research is to examine salivary cortisol as a direct measure of speech state anxiety.

Scholars have identified several arousal systems that are triggered by stress and strain in humans. One system that operates when humans feel state anxiety is the behavior inhibition system (BIS). The BIS increases people's vigilance and sense of alarm. This allows people to respond efficiently and effectively to a stimuli that produces anxiety. Communication researchers have applied the ideas of the BIS to communication apprehension. Highly apprehensive individuals possess a more reactive BIS, as compared to less apprehensive people. Furthermore, people who have highly reactive BIS experience greater physiological arousal during public speaking.

One of the central components of the BIS is the hypothalamus. Specifically, the hypothalamus controls two major neuroendocrine systems: the hypothalamic-pituitary-adrenocortical (HPA) system and the sympathetic-adrenomedullary system. However, only the HPA system is associated with fear and distress. Cortisol is the byproduct of HPA activity and is particularly responsive to stimuli that produce state anxiety. The specific predictions addressed in this study were:

1. The pattern of cortisol levels for public speakers decreases over time.
2. A positive relationship exists between cortisol levels and psychological measure of public speaking state anxiety.

Method

Thirty-one college age students enrolled in a speech communication course participated in an informative speech to an audience of their peers. Two weeks prior to the speech participants were asked to present a five-to-six-minute informative speech, which would be evaluated by their instructor. Participants were instructed to refrain from smoking, physical exercise, foods, alcohol, and caffeine for at least one hour prior to their speech.

All speeches were given between 11 a.m. and 3 p.m. in a standard classroom in front of 20-25 fellow students and an instructor. Speaking order was established by random selection. Following their presentations, speakers went to an adjacent room where saliva samples were taken to test cortisol levels. Additionally, participants completed three measures of state anxiety, one measuring their anxiety during the first minute of their speech, another measuring their anxiety during the last minute of their speech, and another measuring their anxiety one minute after their speech.

Baseline levels of salivary cortisol were taken one week prior to the study. On the day of the presentations, each speaker gave five salivary cortisol samples at eight-minute intervals after the beginning of the speech. Thus, samples were taken at 8, 16, 24, 32, and 40 minutes after the beginning of the speech.

Results

Analyses indicated that salivary cortisol levels decreased over each of the five time periods in a linear fashion. Significant differences were found between the cortisol levels at eight minutes and 40 minutes and for cortisol levels at 16 minutes and 40 minutes.

Salivary cortisol levels were associated with each of the measurements of physiological state anxiety. Specifically, cortisol levels were related to anxiety during the first and last minute of the speech as well as anxiety one minute after the speech. Furthermore, the physiological measures of state anxiety during the act of public speaking were positively correlated with the salivary cortisol levels in all time periods.

Key Ideas

- Psychological stimuli that trigger state anxiety activate the HPA axis of which the stress hormone cortisol is a byproduct.

- After public speaking cortisol levels decrease over time.
- Cortisol levels are associated with measurements of physiological state anxiety.

Chapter Eight: Conflict and Relational Maintenance

In this chapter, we explore research on conflict and maintenance behaviors in personal relationships. The first paper, by Fehm-Wolfsdorf and colleagues, investigates the role that marital quality plays in how large a cortisol response spouses have to marital conflict. Similarly, Kiecolt-Glaser and her co-authors studied changes taking place in new marriages over the course of time and how they are associated with spouses' hormonal changes.

Denton et al. also studied marriage and the patterns of initiating or avoiding conflict discussions, finding that they were related to cardiovascular parameters. Finally, a study by Kaiser and Powers showed that the average testosterone levels in romantic relationships predict male aggression toward female partners.

MARITAL INTERACTION QUALITY INFLUENCES CORTISOL RESPONSES TO MARITAL CONFLICT

Fehm-Wolfsdorf, G., Groth, T., Kaiser, A., & Hahlweg, K. (1999). Cortisol responses to marital conflict depend on marital interaction quality. *International Journal of Behavioral Medicine, 6*, 207-227.

Preview

Couples were videotaped during a marital conflict and then grouped into one of three categories based on their interaction behavior. Specifically, couples displayed either predominantly negative behaviors, positive behaviors, or asymmetric behaviors (one positive and one negative). The overall response to the marital conflict revealed that women had a greater cortisol response than men. With respect to the groups created based on couple interaction behavior, results indicated that couples with a positive interaction demonstrated an increase in cortisol levels, whereas couples with a negative interaction demonstrated a nonresponse in cortisol levels. However, both positive and negative interaction couples rated the conflict discussion as equally stressful.

Description of Study

Although the connection between family relationships and health problems has received increasing attention, researchers have argued that the effects of family – specifically, marital relations – on health are indirect and difficult to understand. The purpose of this study was to examine the direct effect of marital conflict on the stress response and to discover if there are any differences between couples who display different interaction patterns in dealing with conflict.

Past studies of the stress response have examined the cardiovascular, immune, and endocrine systems. However, these studies have found that a response in one system does not necessarily predict a response in another. Studies of cardiovascular response have established a relationship between elevated blood pressure and more negative marital interactions. Furthermore, discussion of marital problems leads to a down-regulation of the immune system in highly negative participants.

Although many studies have examined the effects of stress, these studies have not specifically examined the effect of social stress. Typically, these studies involve cognitive stressors, such as a mental math activity, which involve little or no interpersonal interaction. Researchers argue that the results of the cognitive stress studies cannot be generalized to responses to social stressors. One common source of social stress is conflict within the marital relationship.

Although many studies of marital interaction examine the couple as the unit of interaction, the focus in the present study is on the interdependency of behaviors between the marital partners. The goal in this type of study is to understand the linkages between the behaviors and physiological responses of both couples in comparison to each other. The specific prediction addressed in this study was:

1. Couples with different interaction behaviors exhibit different responses in blood pressure and salivary cortisol.

Method

This study examined cortisol levels, heart rate, and blood pressure in 80 couples. Each couple participated in a two-hour session, all of which took place after 4:30 p.m. to control for diurnal changes in cortisol levels. Furthermore, participants were asked to refrain from alcohol for 24 hours before the session and from food and exercise for the hour preceding the session.

For each session, cortisol, heart rate, and blood pressure were all measured at identical times. Specifically, measurements were taken at 10, 40, 60, 80, and 110 minutes into the session. The first 40 minutes were used as a "warming up" time in which the interviewers asked the couple about the positive aspects of their marriage. Next, participants worked through the Problem List which has each person rate possible problem areas in the marriage such as communication, sexuality, social activity, finances, household chores, jealousy, and alcohol problems. Next subjects participated in a 15-minute videotaped conflict discussion in which the areas of concern from the Problem List were utilized as the impetus for the discussion. During this time the interviewer left the room. Psychological assessments, such as the Partnership Questionnaire, were administered after the discussion, followed by a feedback and debriefing time.

Trained coders reviewed the couples' videotaped conflict discussions using the Coding System for Marital/Family Interaction. The aim of this coding system is to assess the speaking and listening skills of the martial partners. Both verbal and nonverbal behaviors were assessed and categorized as being positive, negative, or neutral behaviors.

Couples were categorized into one of three groups based on their behavior during the conflict discussion. For positive couples, both partners exhibited more positive than negative interaction behaviors. For negative couples, both partners exhibited more negative than positive interaction behaviors. For asymmetrical couples, one partner showed more positive than negative interaction behaviors, whereas the other partner demonstrated more negative than positive interaction behaviors.

Results

Couples who displayed predominantly negative behaviors reported the lowest satisfaction with their marriage. Moreover, couples with predominantly negative interaction reported more quarreling, less tenderness, and less togetherness than positive or asymmetrical couples.

As expected, women had higher cortisol responses to the conflict discussion than men. It is posited that women's higher cortisol responses are due to women's generally higher involvement in the conflict discussion as compared to men.

The cortisol response evoked by the conflict discussion differed between the groups. Couples with predominantly positive interactions showed an increase in cortisol levels, whereas couples with predominantly negative interactions showed a nonresponse in cortisol levels. There was also a difference between women's scores based on the interaction groups. Specifically, wives in positive interactions had a greater cortisol response than wives in negative interactions and wives in asymmetrical interactions had a greater cortisol response than wives in negative interactions. These differences were not found in men.

There was a sex difference in blood pressure, with men having slightly higher systolic and diastolic blood pressure than women. However, there were no differences between the interaction groups for systolic or diastolic blood pressure. Furthermore, there were no differences with respect to heart rate.

Based on this evidence it is argued by the authors that marital interaction quality directly affects both partners physiological response to conflict. Furthermore, these findings support the notion that family relationships can have an influence on health.

Key Ideas

- Couples with predominantly positive interactions had an increase in cortisol levels in response to the conflict discussion.
- Couples with predominantly negative interactions showed a nonresponse in cortisol levels in response to the conflict discussion.
- Women participating in positive and asymmetrical interactions had higher cortisol responses to the conflict discussion than did women in negative interactions.

Newlyweds' Stress Hormones are Related to their Marital Dissolution and Satisfaction Ten Years Later

---

Kiecolt-Glaser, J. K., Bane, C., Glaser, R., & Malarkey, W. B. (2003). Love, marriage, and divorce: Newlyweds' stress hormones foreshadow relationship changes. *Journal of Consulting and Clinical Psychology, 71,* 176-188.

Preview

Stress hormones were assessed in 90 couples participating in a conflict discussion during their first year of marriage and were found to be related to divorce and marital satisfaction ten years later. During a conflict discussion, epinephrine levels of divorced couples at year ten were 34% higher during the first year of marriage than couples who remained married. Furthermore, divorced couples had 22% higher epinephrine levels throughout the day, and both epinephrine and norepinephrine were 16% high at night as compared to married couples. Stress hormone levels in the first year also differentiated between troubled and untroubled marriages ten years later. Specifically, ACTH levels were twice as high in women whose marriages were troubled ten years later than among women whose marriages were untroubled. Couples who were troubled ten years later produced 34% more norepinephrine during conflict, 24% more during the daytime, and 17% more at night than couples who were untroubled.

Description of Study

Communication problems can promote poor marital outcomes. Communication related measures have often been linked to marital dissatisfaction and divorce across a number of studies. However, the results of these studies are often inconsistent. Although communication problems may lead to divorce, other variables may be important in predicting divorce and marital dissatisfaction.

The primary focus of this study was to determine how different personality, experiential, behavioral, and physiological factors can contribute to divorce and marital dissatisfaction. Past research has demonstrated that a relationship exists between particular physiological factors and marital outcomes such as divorce and satisfaction. For example, greater autonomic arousal at baseline was related to declines in marital satisfaction three years later. Moreover, a study of newlywed couples suggested that decreases in the husband's heart rate in response to conflict were related to a lessened probability of divorce six years later.

Generally, exposure to conflict situations typically produces physiological arousal and the subsequent release of stress hormones. This study focused on the stress hormones epinephrine, norepinephrine, cortisol, and ACTH. The question addressed in the current study was how physiological reactivity during a conflict situation relates to marital outcomes. The specific prediction addressed in this study was:

1. Higher levels of stress hormones during and following a problem-solving interaction are related with greater marital instability and lower marital satisfaction ten years later.

Method

This study consisted of 90 newlywed couples who were admitted to a clinical research center (CRC) for a period of 24 hours to give physiological, behavioral, and self-report data. Upon arriving at the CRC, a heparin well (indwelling catheter) was inserted into each participant's arm. After an adaptation period, the couple was then briefly interviewed to determine which topics would be best for the conflict discussion. Couples were then asked to discuss and attempt to resolve the two or three marital issues that the interviewer judged to produce the most conflict. The conflict discussion lasted 30 minutes.

To determine stress hormone levels, blood samples were taken via the heparin well. A baseline sample was taken 90 minutes after the heparin well was inserted. A number of samples was taken during the interview and conflict discussion. Specifically, the first sample was drawn at the end of the 10-20 minute interview and before the conflict discussion. The next samples were drawn 15 minutes after the conflict discussion had started and at the end of the 30-minute conflict discussion. The final sample was drawn at the end of a 15-minute recovery period following the end of the conflict discussion. In addition to these samples, additional samples were acquired hourly from 8 a.m. to 7 p.m. the following day to provide daytime and nighttime values for the four stress hormones (epinephrine, norepinephrine, cortisol, and ACTH).

To determine the satisfaction level of couple the Marital Adjustment Test (MAT) was utilized because of its ability to discriminate between satisfied and dissatisfied couples.

The ten-year follow up involved 100% of the couples in the original sample. Furthermore, the marital status for all the couples was established and marital satisfaction was ascertained for those couples who were still married at the time of the follow up.

Results

Although this study assessed individual differences such as personality and problem-solving behaviors, the strongest and most consistent findings were from the physiological realm. Analysis of the stress hormones revealed that the divorced group showed higher levels of epinephrine during the original experiment than in those who remained married. However, the divorced and married groups did not differ on their levels of norepinephrine. In addition, there were no significant differences between groups on cortisol levels. Divorced couples had higher epinephrine levels throughout the day, and both epinephrine and norepinephrine were higher at night as compared to married couples. Couples who subsequently divorced ten years later differed on three of the four stress hormones assessed during the first year of marriage.

Among couples who were still married, norepinephrine was also significantly higher during the original experiment among those who were classified as dissatisfied ten years later compared to those classified as satisfied. Furthermore, ACTH levels were significantly higher among women whose marriages were troubled ten years later compared to marriages that were untroubled. Couples whose marriages were considered troubled ten years later produced more norepinephrine during conflict, more during the day, and more during the night at the time of the original experiment than marriages that were untroubled.

Although married and divorced couples differed on three of the four stress hormones, they did not diverge significantly on any self-report dimension taken in the first year of their marriage. In particular, there were no differences in marital satisfaction, depression, and levels of hostility.

Key Ideas

- Conflict situations increase the release of stress hormones.

- The relationship between physiological change and negative behaviors during conflict is greater for women than men.

- Divorced couples had higher levels of stress hormones in their first year of marriage compared to couples who were still married.

- Dissatisfied couples had higher levels of stress hormones in their first year of marriage compared to couples who were satisfied.

Avoiding Marital Conflict Relates to Higher Blood Pressure Reactivity

---

Denton, W. H., Burleson, B. R., Hobbs, B. V., Von Stein, M., & Rodriguez, C. P. (2001). Cardiovascular reactivity and initiate/avoid patterns of marital communication: A test of Gottman's psychophysiologic model of marital interaction. *Journal of Behavioral Medicine, 24,* 401-421.

Preview

Psychologist John Gottman created the psychophysiologic model of marital interaction, which predicts varying sex responses, both psychologically and physiologically, during a conflict scenario. The current study tested this model, using 60 married couples, classifying participants as either initiators or avoiders of conflict. During the session, couples were taken through several stress-inducing situations (including a combined interview). Heart rate and blood pressure were measured throughout. Compared to initiators, avoiders were found to have greater systolic blood pressure (BP) reactivity through the interview. Husbands of avoider wives showed greater BP reactivity than husbands of initiator wives. Finally, the greatest amount of systolic BP reactivity was found in initiator husbands of avoider wives.

Description of Study

The concept of cardiovascular reactivity (changes in cardiovascular functions due to various stressors) has been linked to various health risks, including heart disease and hypertension. There also appears to be a sex difference, as men experience greater blood pressure reactivity than women (though this is stronger for diastolic than systolic blood pressure). To explain this, Gottman created the psychophysiologic model of marital interaction, stating that sex differences in cardiovascular reactivity would coincide with sex differences of marital communication. The model argues that husbands, when physiologically aroused, will withdraw from marital conflict. That withdrawal, in turn, will physiologically arouse the wife, who will attempt to reengage the husband in the conflict. Basically, physiological arousal causes men to avoid conflict, while physiological arousal causes women to initiate conflict.

In the few studies that have empirically tested Gottman's model, husbands with high levels of hostility were found to have greater systolic blood pressure reactivity when influencing their wives. In addition, hypertensive women experience an increase in blood pressure during a hostile marriage discussion. However, no studies have tested the actual initiate-avoid pattern provided in the model. Toward that end, this study proposed that the initiate-avoid pattern would be positively related to cardiovascular reactivity, with sex not having a significant effect. Specifically, the study predicted:

1. Individuals (men or women) who avoid marital problem discussions show greater amounts of cardiovascular reactivity than individuals who initiate the discussions.

Method

The researchers recruited participants in 60 married couples. Participants had a mean age of 39 years and had been married an average of 12 years. The participant couples came together to a lab session, abstaining from caffeine, alcohol, and tobacco for a specific period of time prior to the session. First, the participants separately completed questionnaires, which comprised of the Dyadic Adjustment Scale (measuring marital adjustment), the Positive Feelings Questionnaire (measuring positive feelings toward the spouse), and the Beck Depression Inventory (measuring self-reported depression). Blood pressure of the participants was taken every minute.

The participants were then put through a series of stressors designed to heighten cardiovascular functions and psychological stress. First, participants were instructed to place their hands in a container of ice water for 45 to 75 seconds. Second, participants were asked to subtract seven from 2018 continually for 5 minutes. Research assistants monitored the arithmetic, looking for quickness and accuracy in the results, further stressing the participants. Finally, participants were required to watch 5 minutes of a video showing couples arguing, with instructions to imagine that they were involved in the conflict. Blood pressure and heart rate was measured at various times throughout all procedures.

After the stressors, the couples were reunited and interviewed by a researcher, with the questions designed to show the pattern of initiate-avoid tactics performed by either spouse. Couples were forced to confront divisive issues in their relationship, responding to interview questions detailing whether they would bring up the issues, if one person would be more likely to bring it up, and what specific response would be used. The interviewer would then ensure that both individuals agreed on who initiated and who avoided on each particular issue. The communication and behavior of the interview was then coded, to classifying one person as the initiator and the other as the avoider.

Results

There were 46 avoiders (31 male, 15 female) and 70 initiators (27 male, 43 female) in the sample. Coders classified seven avoid-avoid couples, 21 initiate-initiate couples, 23 female initiate/male avoid couples, and 7 male initiate/female avoid couples. Overall, the study showed support for Gottman's model, though the findings also differed from the model in key ways. First, men were more likely than women to be avoiders, whereas women were more likely than men to be initiators during the interview. The psychophysiologic model explains this finding by stating that men experience a higher amount of physiologic reactivity, thus withdrawing from the interaction. However, this study found that men actually had lower systolic and diastolic reactivity than did women, whereas men had higher baseline blood pressure. This was seemingly contradictory to Gottman's model.

The current study also supported Gottman's model by finding that avoiders experienced significantly greater amounts of cardiovascular reactivity than did initiators. This supports the idea that avoidance was used to lessen the unpleasant experience of the physiological arousal. Once again, however, the study found that the avoider-initiator construct is more complex than a simple sex difference. For example, husbands who related to avoider wives had significantly greater reactivity than husbands who related to initiator wives, especially when the husband himself was an initiator. Basically, sex does not appear to be as influential as the avoider-initiator role. Consequently, Gottman's model seemingly relates more to the avoider-initiator roles than to sex. Either sex can be the initiator, and either can be the avoider, and it is the combination of the two spouses that appears to affect cardiovascular reactivity. Future studies should specifically examine whether specific patterns of marital communication create lower baseline readings of cardiovascular activity (as well as reactivity).

Key Ideas

- Avoiding spouses had greater amounts of cardiovascular reactivity than initiating spouses.

- The avoider-initiator role of the spouse (instead of sex) appears to have a significant role in predicting cardiovascular reactivity in a discussion about conflicts in the relationship.

Dyadic Testosterone Levels Predict Male Aggression and Physical Assault toward Female Partners

---

Kaiser, H., & Powers, S. (2006). Testosterone and conflict tactics within late-adolescent couples: A dyadic predictive model. *Journal of Social and Personal Relationships, 23*, 231-248.

Preview

This study hypothesized that dyadic (male and female) testosterone levels would predict the amount of aggressive behavior in a relationship. Participants filled out a questionnaire detailing aspects of their relationship, and gave a saliva sample to measure the steroid hormone testosterone. Findings indicated that aggressive behavior of the man was higher when the testosterone levels of the two partners were similar (both partners had either high or low levels of testosterone) than when they were dissimilar (one partner had high levels, and the other had low levels). Women's testosterone level moderated the man's aggressive tendencies, which is interesting because previous work had only linked a man's aggression with his own testosterone level.

Description of Study

Compared to women, men experience greater intensity and more variability in testosterone levels, strengthening the relationships between testosterone and behavior. For example, adolescent boys' testosterone levels provided a direct link to provoked aggressive behavior. Previous studies have also linked the struggle for dominance to testosterone levels, concluding that boys would not respond indiscriminately, but would quickly move to defend themselves against a perceived threat to their social power. These studies provide important information about the nature of conflict in romantic relationships, wherein power imbalances are negotiated frequently between partners.

For marital relationships, high testosterone in men was linked to low marital satisfaction and higher divorce rates. However, scholars are beginning to study whether these results are due solely to the level of testosterone or the interplay between the testosterone levels of the two partners. Recent research finds that women are the main source of aggression (both psychologically and physically) in a relationship, in sharp contrast to the stereotypically quiet wife. Although women are typically more aggressive in marital relationships than men, women still receive a greater amount of physical violence (a heightened form of aggression). This study sought to better understand how the testosterone levels of both partners, instead of just the man's, predicted relational aggression. The specific predictions of the study were:

1. The higher the testosterone levels are for women, and the lower the testosterone levels are for men, the less aggression (both psychologically and physically) that occurs in the relationship.
2. The higher the testosterone levels are for men, and the lower the testosterone levels are for women, the more men use aggressive behaviors (both psychologically and physically).

Method

Researchers recruited 90 heterosexual late-adolescent couples, ranging from 18-20 years old. Participants were required to visit the laboratory with their relational partner, after not drinking or using drugs for the 24 hours prior to the visit, and not exercising or smoking 2 hours prior in order to achieve accurate hormonal readings. When the participants reached the lab, they were separated from their partners and told to fill out an admissions questionnaire detailing any activity or illness that would affect the measurement of testosterone. Directly after completing that task, participants gave a saliva sample. The participants then filled out measures detailing the usage of conflict tactics such as psychological and physical aggression. Only the subscales focusing on minor psychological (insulting, swearing) and physical (pushing, throwing objects) forms of aggressive behavior were analyzed.

Results

Overall, women and men showed no significant differences in the use of both psychological and physical forms of aggressive behavior. As expected, the men did have a significantly higher level of testosterone. Women were a little less likely to use physical aggression (1.30 times per year vs. 1.96 times per year for men), and the use of physical aggression by one partner was positively correlated with the use of physical aggression by the other partner. Most important, men whose partners had similar testosterone levels were more likely to commit physical aggression than men whose partners had dissimilar testosterone levels.

Key Ideas

- In romantic couples, similar levels of testosterone predicted higher amounts of both psychological and physical acts of aggression for men.
- In romantic couples, dissimilar levels of testosterone predicted lower amounts of both psychological and physical acts of aggression for men.

Chapter Nine: Emotion

Humans experience a full range of emotions and our physiology is often intricately involved in those emotional experiences. In this chapter, Turner et al. investigate the role of distressing emotions in the secretion of oxytocin. Richman and colleagues, by contrast, examine the benefits of positive emotion on health and the development of disease.

Martin and colleagues look at a specific emotion — depression — and study its relationship with digit length in men (which is believed to be an indicator of testosterone level). Finally, Floyd and Mikkelson look at the ability to accurately decode facial displays of emotion and the role played by neurological hemispheric dominance in this process.

Plasma Oxytocin Levels are Linked to Emotion and Interpersonal Distress

---

Turner, R.A., Altemus, M., Enos, T., Cooper, B., & McGuinness, T. (1999). Preliminary research on plasma oxytocin in normal cycling women: Investigating emotion and interpersonal distress. *Psychiatry, 62*, 97-113.

Preview

Recent research has linked the hormone oxytocin to attachment and maternal behavior in animals. This study sought to understand if a similar relationship between oxytocin and maternal behavior existed in humans. Twenty-five women participated in a study investigating oxytocin responsivity to three different interventions, including massage, positive emotion, and negative emotion. The researchers found that oxytocin levels in the women appeared to rise after the massage intervention, while they fell after the negative emotion intervention. Women who were currently in a romantic relationship showed a stronger increase in oxytocin after the positive emotion intervention than did single women. Consequently, these results appear to show a link between oxytocin and several emotional and behavioral characteristics in women.

Description of Study

Oxytocin is a hormone normally found in mammalian lactation and orgasm, and is found in significantly higher amounts in women than in men. Most previous research involving nonhuman mammals has found a strong relationship between oxytocin levels and maternal behaviors such as offspring acceptance and nurturing. These studies also show that oxytocin is a stimulant for sexual attraction to a specific partner as well as a mechanism for alleviating distress in animal babes separated from their mothers.

Whereas the human brain involves numerous receptors for oxytocin, little is known about how the hormone affects human behavior and interaction. Researchers believe that oxytocin could promote attachment behaviors, sexual activity, maternal impulses, and cause warm, pleasant feelings for the individual. Unfortunately, previous research on oxytocin in humans is sparse and conflicting. For example, one study found a negative correlation between baseline oxytocin levels and aggression and guilt, whereas another found a positive correlation between baseline oxytocin levels and aggression and guilt. A third study found no relationship between these variables.

The current study attempted to clarify this confliction in previous research by examining oxytocin reactivity (change due to a stimulus) instead of simply studying baseline oxytocin levels. The authors argued that the change in oxytocin levels could be of greater importance than baseline oxytocin levels for spurring positive behavioral outcomes. Thus, the goals of the study were to both develop guidelines for studying oxytocin in future research, as well as derive some introductory data on oxytocin reactivity. The researchers used three stimulants in the study; a positive emotional state associated with attachment, relaxation massage, and a negative emotional state associated with attachment. The researchers also proposed that various psychological traits related to adult attachment and women's perceptions of their own childhood relationship with their caregivers would moderate the oxytocin responsivity to the three stimulants. For example, the researchers predicted that a woman who had a negative perception of her childhood caregiver would show a stronger amount of oxytocin reactivity for the negative emotional intervention. The study specifically predicted:

1. Participants with greater oxytocin reactivity in response to positive emotion and relaxation massage report fewer interpersonal problems and a more positive attachment history with caregivers than participants with a smaller oxytocin response.

Method

Researchers recruited 26 normally ovulating women (24 were used) for a study on hormones and personality. 56% of the participants were currently in a romantic relationship, with a mean age of 28 years. Participants initially were screened for various psychological and behavioral problems, as well as their most recent sexual behavior. All sessions began at 8:30 AM, lasting for about three hours, with participants fasting the morning before the session. The participants were seated in a comfortable chair, with a catheter placed in the nondominant arm. After an introductory time of 45 minutes, for the participants to become used to the catheter, two baseline blood draws were taken 15 minutes apart. All participants were put through the three stimuli described above in a counterbalanced order. The massage stimulus was undertaken by a female massage therapist to use Swedish massage techniques on the participants' neck and shoulders for 15 minutes. The positive and negative emotion stimuli were both completed by giving the participants instructions to imagine an important past experience where they felt love/infatuation (for the positive emotion stimulus) or sad/loss/abandonment (for the negative emotion stimulus). Nine more blood draws were taken during and between the three stimuli. Finally, the participants completed a questionnaire, which addressed the participants' perception of their childhood relationship with their caregivers, an inventory of interpersonal problems, and adult attachment.

Results

Several interesting conclusions were derived from this study. First, baseline oxytocin readings were positively related to aspects of interpersonal distress, including intrusiveness, anxiety, and coldness. Women who were not currently in a romantic relationship had higher baseline oxytocin readings than women who were currently in a romantic relationship.

Participants showed an increase in oxytocin levels in relation to the massage stimuli, and showed a decrease in relation to the negative emotion stimuli (showing a clear link between oxytocin and emotions). Surprisingly, no relation was found between oxytocin levels and the positive emotion stimuli. However, the participants that showed a greater increase of oxytocin in response to the massage stimuli did show an increase in response to the positive emotion stimuli. Finally, women who had larger positive increases in oxytocin during the positive emotion stimuli were more likely to be in a romantic relationship than those with smaller positive increases, which the researchers claim could be due to the general frequency of sexual activity.

Those same participants (who showed positive responses to both massage and positive emotion), as well as participants who did not show a decrease in oxytocin in response to the negative emotion stimuli, were less likely than the rest of the sample to be instrusive, finding it difficult to stay out of other people's business. The possible conclusion for this finding is that women who have a greater amount of oxytocin available during happy times and experience a smaller oxytocin decrease during sad times experience greater satisfaction in interpersonal relationships than women with a lesser amount of available oxytocin. Oxytocin increases during the positive emotion stimuli was also negatively related with the interpersonal problem of overly nurturing behavior. Further, oxytocin decreases during the negative emotion stimuli was positively related to anxiety in close relationships. The researchers argue that future research should perhaps focus on the frequency of oxytocin pulses into the bloodstream.

Key Ideas

- Oxytocin levels fell in response to the negative emotion stimuli.
- Oxytocin levels rose in response to the massage stimuli.
- Participants who showed a greater positive response to the massage stimuli also showed a positive response to the positive emotion stimuli.
- Participants who showed a greater positive response to the positive emotion stimuli were more likely to currently be in a romantic relationship.

HIGH LEVELS OF HOPE AND CURIOSITY DECREASE LIKELIHOOD OF DEVELOPING DISEASES

Richman, L. S., Kubzansky, L., Maselko, J., Kawachi, I., Choo, P., & Bauer, M. (2005). Positive emotion and health: Going beyond the negative. *Health Psychology, 24,* 422-429.

Preview

Few studies have examined the effect of positive emotions on the human body. In this study, researchers proposed that trait levels of hope and curiosity would decrease the likelihood of developing three diseases, including hypertension, diabetes mellitus, and respiratory tract infections. Self-report questionnaires were measured against medical data gathered over a 2-year period. High trait levels of hope significantly decreased the likelihood of developing all three diseases, whereas high trait levels of curiosity significantly decreased the likelihood of developing hypertension and diabetes mellitus. Researchers posit that positive emotions might serve as a buffer against disease by strengthening the immune system.

Description of Study

Researchers have long been interested in the relationship between negative emotions and health, discovering associations between negative emotions such as anger or anxiety and diseases such as diabetes, cardiovascular disease, and asthma. In fact, recent research lends strength to the notion that negative emotions help cause various diseases, including diabetes and hypertension. For example, individuals with high anxiety in one study were twice as likely to develop hypertension as were those with less anxiety. Negative emotions are also related to negative health behaviors (smoking, drinking, obesity, and lack of exercise). In response, numerous models have attempted to explain the relationship between emotion and health.

The current study focuses on the benefits of positive emotions such as hope and curiosity. Hope, in particular, builds optimism in meeting future expectations, and is positively related to mental health, quality of life, and survival times for cancer patients. Curiosity, on the other hand, encourages investigation and novelty, engaging individuals in the world around them. Curiosity also appears to be positively related to survival for older individuals. For this study, hope and curiosity were assessed for their association with three physician-diagnosed diseases: hypertension, diabetes mellitus, and respiratory tract infection. The specific prediction of the study was:

1. Positive emotions (hope and curiosity) protect against hypertension, diabetes mellitus, and respiratory tract infection.

Method

The researchers randomly selected 5,500 patients from a healthcare practice serving over 180,000 adults. The physician of the patient was contacted and asked for permission to contact the patient. Since some physicians did not grant consent, 4,027 questionnaires were sent out to participants, and the researchers received 1,041 responses. The time of the questionnaire was treated as the midpoint in the study. Thus, one year after the questionnaire was returned, the researchers computed data from medical records, focusing on the pre-baseline period of the year prior to questionnaire completion, as well as the post-baseline period of the year after questionnaire completion. The questionnaire itself ascertained trait levels of hope and curiosity, along with the negative emotions of anger and anxiety. Participants were asked to detail health related behaviors and demographic information.

Two physicians, unaware of participant emotional scores, developed the categories for the three diseases. Each participant received a "yes" or "no" for the prevalence of both hypertension and diabetes mellitus (determining whether the participant had been diagnosed within the two-year time frame). Each participant also received a "yes" or "no" for the incidence of both diseases (determining whether the participant had been diagnosed post-baseline). Four diseases were classified as respiratory tract infections: acute respiratory infections, acute bronchitis, pneumonia, and bronchitis. Since these diseases are not chronic, the outcome measure simply counted the number of times the participant had been diagnosed with any respiratory tract infection over the two-year period.

Results

As predicted, the trait level of positive emotions, even after controlling for health behaviors, was negatively related to numerous health outcomes for participants. Importantly, these outcomes ranged across cardiovascular, metabolic, and respiratory health functions. Specifically, curiosity was strongly negatively related to incidence and prevalence rates of hypertension, as well as prevalence rates of diabetes mellitus. Hope was strongly negatively rated to prevalence rates of hypertension, prevalence rates of diabetes mellitus, and the number of respiratory tract infections. The negative emotions of anger and anxiety were mostly unrelated to the health outcomes, with anger predicting only the prevalence of diabetes mellitus.

Overall, these findings lend support to the idea that positive emotions can serve as a buffer against diseases. Although a relationship between positive emotions and health appears to exist, the various mechanisms of this relationship still remain unexplored. For example, positive emotions might actually boost immune performance. It is also possible that individuals who are generally positive are also more likely than others to pay attention to health measures and health information. Further, positive individuals may have more relationships, allowing more access to resources that spur knowledge. Finally, positive emotions might help lessen the physiological impact of stress, as individuals who are generally more positive might not experience stress as sharply as those who are more negative. This study supports the notion that positive emotions are not simply the absence of negative emotions, but appear to serve an important physiological function by themselves.

Key Ideas

- Trait levels of hope are negatively related to prevalence rates of hypertension and diabetes, along with the number of respiratory tract infections.
- Trait levels of curiosity are negatively related to incidence and prevalence rates of hypertension, along with prevalence rates of diabetes.
- Positive emotions might serve as a buffer against disease, helping to strengthen the immune system.

FLUCTUATING ASYMMETRY AND DIGIT LENGTH ARE RELATED TO DEPRESSION IN MEN

Martin, S. M., Manning, J. T., & Dowrick, C. F. (1999). Fluctuating asymmetry, relative digit length, and depression in men. *Evolution and Human Behavior, 20,* 203-214.

Preview

The purpose of this work was to examine the possible connection between fluctuating asymmetry and depression, and the link between finger length (which is a marker of prenatal testosterone) and depression. Results indicated that depression was positively related to fluctuating asymmetry in men but not in women. In addition, finger length, particularly the fourth digit, was positively related to depression in men but not in women.

Description of Study

Humans have a developmental plan that gets executed to varying degrees of precision. Deviations from the developmental plan can happen due to genetic and physiological stressors such as mutations, chromosomal aberrations, testosterone, and corticosteroids, in addition to environmental stressors such as pollution and infection. Studies of humans and nonhumans have revealed that high developmental stability (i. e., few developmental deviations) is associated with disease resistance, athleticism, and fertility.

Developmental instability is most commonly measured as fluctuating asymmetry. Asymmetry, in the form of small deviations from perfect symmetry, has been shown to be a negative indicator of developmental stability. Specifically, facial asymmetry has been found to be positively correlated with measures of depression.

Prenatal testosterone is essential to testicular development, but it may also lead to dyslexia, autism, stammering, migraine, and a reduction in the functioning of the immune system. Thus, while testosterone is essential for male development, it also represents a stressor to the development of the central nervous system. Some researchers have suggested that finger length may be a marker of prenatal testosterone levels. In men, testosterone levels have been found to be related to the length of the fourth digit. Specifically, men with high testosterone tend to have a fourth digit that is longer than the second, whereas men with low testosterone tend to have a fourth digit that is shorter than the second. The specific predictions addressed in this study were:

1. Depression is correlated with fluctuating asymmetry.
2. Depression is correlated with digit length, particularly that of the fourth digit.

Method

The study tested depression, fluctuating asymmetry, and digit length in 52 men and 50 women. An attempt was made to include nondepressed and depressed participants in the study, so as to increase the variance of the sample. Depression was assessed using the revised Beck Depression Inventory.

Finger length was measured using the second through the fifth digit on both hands. This was measured from the basal crease of the digit to the tip. Fluctuating asymmetry was also measured using digit length in addition to the diameter of the wrists, and ear height. The asymmetry for each trait was calculated by subtracting the size of the right side from the size of the left side. Absolute fluctuating asymmetry scores were calculated by removing the signs from the scores, correcting for trait size, then summing the scores and dividing by the total number of traits that were measured.

Results

Depression was positively related to fluctuating asymmetry in men as asymmetric men reported more depression than symmetric men. However, there was no relationship between depression and fluctuating asymmetry in women.

Depression was positively related to digit length in men. This relationship was strongest for the fourth digit on both hands. Other predictors of depression for men were the second digit on the right hand, second digit on the left hand, and the third digit on the left hand. There was no relationship between depression and digit length in women.

Digit length corrected for height (digit length divided by height) was a stronger predictor depression in men than digit length alone. As before, the fourth digit exhibited the strongest relationship with depression. All other digits corrected for height were related to depression except for the fifth digit on the left hand. There was no relationship between depression and digit length (corrected for height) in women.

Key Ideas

- Fluctuating asymmetry is a marker of developmental deviation and instability.
- In men, testosterone levels have been found to be related to the length of the fourth digit.
- Depression was related to fluctuating asymmetry in men but not in women.
- Digit length, particularly the fourth digit, was positively related to depression in men but not in women.

Brain Dominance and Sex Interact to Influence Accuracy of Decoding Facial Displays of Emotion

---

Floyd, K., & Mikkelson, A. C. (2003). Effects of brain laterality on accuracy of decoding facial displays of emotion. *Communication Quarterly, 51*, 417-435.

Preview

The primary nonverbal channel for the communication of emotion is the human face, which is capable of producing a large variety of unique expressions. This study examined the effects of neurological hemispheric dominance and sex on the ability to accurately decode facial displays of emotion. Participants were classified as standard, mixed, or anomalous dominant based on multiple measures. Consistent with past research, the researchers found that hemispheric dominance and sex interacted to influence the participants' abilities to accurately decode facial displays of emotions. Specifically, mixed dominant females had the highest accuracy, whereas mixed dominant males had the lowest accuracy.

Description of Study

The human face is a remarkably communicative instrument that can produce a large number of unique expressions that can effectively convey information about the sender's attitudes, cognitions, and moods. One of the primary communicative functions of the face is the expression of emotion. Facial displays of emotion are often representative of people's underlying thoughts, emotions, and physical states. Thus, the ability to decode facial displays of emotion accurately can provide an advantage to the decoder. For example, if a person displays the emotion of fear in a dangerous situation, then those who can accurately decode that display should be better able to avoid the dangerous situation than those who can't accurately decode that facial display of emotion.

This study proposed that one characteristic that may affect people's ability to decode facial displays of emotion is their neurological hemispheric dominance, or whether one is "left brained," "right brained," or has mixed hemispheric dominance. Specifically, the decoding of any message is controlled by the information processing of the brain. Thus, differences in how information is processed in the brain could influence the decoding of communicative messages in general, and facial displays of emotion, in particular.

In most human brains language or verbal communication is function of the left hemisphere, whereas spatial skills and nonverbal communication is function of the right hemisphere. Furthermore, each hemisphere has a particular style in which it processes information. In most people the left hemisphere processes information in a logical manner, whereas the left hemisphere processes information in an emotion and holistic manner. Furthermore, the left hemisphere is adept at determining the literal meaning of information, whereas the right hemisphere is adept at determining the implied meaning of information.

Although these differences between brain hemispheres hold for a majority of people, some people have a different pattern of brain dominance. According to Geschwind and Galaburda, the common brain specialization (left for verbal and right for nonverbal) is known as standard hemispheric dominance (SD). In people not demonstrating SD, these functions of the brain might be symmetrically shared across hemispheres, or they might be reversed (right for verbal and left for nonverbal). These individuals demonstrate what is known as anomalous dominance (AD). Geschwind and Galaburda estimate that approximately 70% of the population exhibits SD and 30% exhibits AD. Some people cannot be reliably be categorized as having standard or anomalous dominance and are considered to have mixed dominance

(MD). Mixed dominance is a default category for those who have the marker characteristics of both SD and AD.

Finally, research indicates that there are sex differences in hemispheric dominance. However, the nature and size of these differences is still not completely understood by researchers, as results have been inconsistent. The specific questions addressed in this study were:

1. Does hemispheric dominance affect the decoding of facially expressed emotion?
2. Does hemispheric dominance and sex interact to affect the decoding of facially expressed emotion?
3. How, if at all, is decoding accuracy for displays of facial emotion affected by the specific emotion being displayed?

Method

Three tests were used in combination to determine the hemispheric dominance of each participant. The first test was a handedness inventory, which assessed the extent to which participants were right-handed, left-handed, or ambidextrous. The second test was a family handedness inventory, which assessed the handedness of the participants' mother, father, brothers, and sisters. Finally, a learning and immune disorder inventory assessed whether participants had been diagnosed and/or treated for learning and immune disorders. These tests were used because each of these markers has been strongly linked with brain laterality. Participants were marked as either SD, AD, or MD for each individual test. If at least two of the three tests showed the same result, then that participant was labeled as having that type of dominance. For example, if at least two of the tests showed that a participant was AD; then he or she was considered AD for the study. If all three tests were different (one SD, one AD, and one MD) then the participant was labeled MD.

Decoding ability for facial displays of emotion was assessed using the Facial Meaning Sensitivity Test. This instrument uses a series of ten photographs, each depicting a young woman's facial expression of a particular emotion. The names of ten corresponding emotions were listed and the participant was asked to match the name of the emotion with the picture in which that emotion was being displayed. The ten emotions were: disgust, happiness, interest, sadness, bewilderment, contempt, surprise, anger, determination, and fear.

Results

The results indicate that hemispheric dominance and sex interacted to influence the participants' abilities to accurately decode facial displays of emotions. Specifically, MD females had the highest accuracy (69.8%), whereas MD males had the lowest accuracy (59.2%). Furthermore, MD females (69.8%) were significantly more accurate than SD males (60.5%). The following is the rank ordering for each group from highest to lowest accuracy: MD females (69.8%), AD males (67.8%), AD females (66.5%), SD females (66.4%), SD males (60.5%), MD males (59.2%).

Moreover, individuals decoded displays of basic emotions (happiness, sadness, anger, fear, surprise) more accurately than displays of complex emotions (interest, bewilderment, determination, contempt, disgust). Overall, participants correctly decoded displays of basic emotions 94.1% of the time, as compared to 35.4% for displays of complex emotions.

Key Ideas

- People process information differently depending on their hemispheric dominance.

- In standard dominant individuals, the left hemisphere primarily processes verbal communication and the right hemisphere primarily processes nonverbal communication.

- In anomalous dominant individuals, these processes are either shared across hemispheres or reversed (left for nonverbal, right for verbal).

- Sex and hemispheric dominance both play an important role in understanding how we decode facial displays of emotion.

- People decode displays of basic emotions more accurately than displays of complex emotions.

Chapter Ten: Attraction

Interpersonal attraction is important because it is often what initiates the development of personal relationships. The papers in this chapter study attraction from a variety of perspectives. First, Thornhill and Gangestad test the notion that men with greater physical symmetry are perceived by normally ovulating women to smell more attractive than more asymmetrical men. Pierce and colleagues then examine how people's relationship potential is predicted by their response to two specific odors.

Feinberg et al.'s study finds that women's facial attractiveness and facial femininity are predicted by the average pitch of their voices. Similarly, Shackelford and Larsen found, in their study, that facial attractiveness is predictive of physical health.

SYMMETRICAL MEN SMELL BETTER THAN ASYMMETRICAL MEN TO NORMALLY OVULATING WOMEN

Thornhill, R., & Gangestad, S. W. (1999). The scent of symmetry: A human sex pheromone that signals fitness? *Evolution and Human Behavior, 20,* 175-201.

Preview

Previous research by the authors discovered that women rated the scent of men with bilateral body symmetry as most attractive when at the fertile height of the menstrual cycle. This study replicates that finding, adding various control measures into the analysis, including the hygiene of the men. In the present study, women rated facial attractiveness highest when at the fertile height of the menstrual cycle. Men, on the other hand, were discovered to have no preference for the scent of more symmetrical women, leading to the conclusion that scent attraction is more powerful for women than for men. Importantly, for both sexes, scent predicted facial attractiveness for the opposite sex, supporting the notion that physical attraction is a multi-faceted construct.

Description of Study

Whereas human attraction is a complicated process for most of us, recent research supports the idea that body odors influence ratings of attraction. In previous research, women have rated olfactory information to be the most important source of attraction, whereas men rated visual and olfactory information to be equally relevant. Importantly, it also appears that the menstrual cycle for normal ovulating women (those who do not use birth control pills) affects their reactions to scents. For example, when confronted with the common scent androstenone over various phases of the menstrual cycle, women rated the scent as most positive when ovulating (the fertile peak of the cycle). Ovulating women also had the highest positive reaction to androstenol (a musky-smelling scent that appears to be connected to sexual selection) when compared with women at other stages in the menstrual cycle. In fact, sexual interest and desire for women is also connected to ovulation, leading to the premise that scent is one adaptive technique for women in choosing a proper mate with better genes.

As stated earlier, the authors conducted an earlier study discovering that women at the height of their menstrual cycle reported greater attraction to the scent of more symmetrical men. The current study sought to replicate those findings and extend them in three specific ways. First, the current study controlled for potential confounding variables in the analysis, including the amount of hygiene performed by the man. Second, the study examined whether women would prefer the scent of more visually facial attractive men, along with more symmetrical men. Finally, the study investigated whether men would also prefer the scent of more symmetrical women. The specific prediction of the study was:

1. Men's FA correlates more negatively with attractiveness ratings made by high-fertility-risk women than with those made by low-fertility-risk women.

Method

Researchers recruited 162 participants (80 men, 82 women) from an introductory psychology course. Participants came to an initial lab session in same-sex groups of four, filling out a questionnaire detailing demographic information. They were measured twice for several aspects of body symmetry, including ear length, wrist width, ankle width, foot breadth, and the length of all fingers except the thumb. Researchers also photographed the face of the participant. Finally, each participant was given a new, clean T-shirt and a set of instructions regarding the next few days. They were required to wear the T-shirt at night for the next two days, cleaning their sheets with unscented laundry detergent beforehand. During the two days, the participants were not allowed to use certain products, such as scented soap or any fragrance. They were forbidden to eat strong-scented food such as garlic, strong cheese, or yogurt, and could not drink alcohol or smoke. They could also not sleep with or have sex with another person during the two days. The T-shirt was placed in a plastic bag during the day, and returned to the researchers the morning of the third day. After returning the T-shirt, they filled out a brief questionnaire asking if they had followed the instructions.

All participants reported to the lab for a second session on the morning of the third day. Each participant was placed in a separate room to rate approximately ten of the T-shirts worn by the opposite-sex, with the addition of one T-shirt that had not been worn. Raters smelled each shirt, rating each by intensity, pleasantness, and sexiness. Women raters also were asked about where they were in their menstrual cycle. A few T-shirts smelled of smoke and other fragrances, and were discarded by the researchers. Finally, the researchers recruited an additional 14 women and 15 men to rate the photographs of the opposite sex for facial attractiveness. The facial attractiveness scores for each photograph were combined, creating one score of attractiveness for each participant.

Results

As predicted, women who were at the height of their menstrual cycle showed a positive association with male body symmetry and scent attractiveness, even controlling for men who showered more or used fragrances. Also, as predicted, women who were at the height of their menstrual cycle showed a positive association between the attraction to the scent of men and greater facial attractiveness. However, there appears to be no relationship between the scent of a woman with low FA and male attraction, although there was a positive correlation between a woman's scent attractiveness to men and facial attractiveness.

Overall, these findings lend support to the belief that women have a specific preference for the scent of men at a particular time at their menstrual cycle, with scent playing a significant role for sexual and mate selection. These findings also provide additional evidence that body symmetry and odor are two signs of men possessing excellent genetic material, which leads to opposite-sex attraction. This is especially true for women since pair-bonding limits the individuals who will provide the genes for children, so women should use these guidelines in initially choosing a sexual partner. Other possible explanations include that symmetrical men are seen as better protectors of women and offspring, that symmetrical men have more adequate sperm, and that symmetrical men have a better functioning immune system.

Key Ideas

- Women at the height of their menstrual cycle prefer the scent of men with greater body symmetry.
- Women at the height of their menstrual cycle prefer the scent of men with greater facial attractiveness.
- The relationship between scent and attraction appears to be stronger for women than for men.

Human Responsiveness to Two Odors Affects Potential for Interpersonal Relationships

---

Pierce, J. D., Cohen, A. B., & Ulrich, P. M. (2004). Responsiveness to two oderants, androstenone and amyl acetate, and the affective impact of odors on interpersonal relationships. *Journal of Comparative Psychology, 118,* 14–19.

Preview

Previous research shows contradictory information regarding the effects of various odors on interpersonal attraction. The Affective Impact of Odor Scale (AIO) was developed to study whether odors, in general, impacted an individual's preferences for particular people, places, or things. However, the scale did not pinpoint any particular odor as a culprit. The current study examined two potential human pheromones, androstenone and amyl acetate, measuring the relationship between an individual's responsiveness (sensitivity) to the two odors with the self-report of the AIO scale. In general, participants with greater responsiveness to androstenone reported a negative effect on interpersonal relationships, whereas participants with greater responsiveness to amyl acetate reported a positive effect on interpersonal relationships.

Description of Study

The current study correlated individual responsiveness to two specific human pheromones (androstenone and amyl acetate) and self-reports of attraction (using the AIO scale). As a pheromone, androstenone (which is generally regarded as a foul odor) is believed to influence human attraction. Thus, this study proposed that individual difference in responsiveness to androstenone would potentially moderate olfactory influences on human moods and social interactions. The study also used amyl acetate, a pleasant smelling odor, as a potential counterpoint to androstenone. The specific predictions of the study were:

1. Individuals sensitive to androstenone report stronger negative effects of odors on interpersonal relationships than individuals insensitive to androstenone.
2. Individuals sensitive to amyl acetate report stronger positive effects of odors on interpersonal relationships than individuals insensitive to amyl acetate.

Method

Researchers recruited 258 undergraduate students from the University of Pennsylvania in the study. One third of the participants reported being in a long-term romantic relationship. First, each participant completed the AIO, measuring the importance of odors on interpersonal relationships in various contexts. They were then instructed to sniff the two odorants, which were contained in squeeze bottles with plastic flip-up lids. After the participant had smelled both odors, they rated the intensity and pleasantness of the odor on a scale from 1 to 9.

Results

The AIO was split into two totaled subscales, where four answers dealt with positive reactions to smell (becoming the Positive Smells factor) and four answers dealt with negative reactions to smell (becoming the Negative Smells factor). The Positive Smells factor had a mean of 12.4 (out of 20), while the Negative Smells factor had a mean of 10.4. No participants rated the intensity of amyl acetate below a 2, and thus the researchers classified no one as anosmic to the scent. However, 55 participants (21% total, 35 men, 20 women) were classified as anosmic to androstenone, rating the intensity of androstenone with a 1.

The AIO scores were then analyzed using multiple regression analysis with the odor responsiveness scores and gender. Consistent with previous research, gender had no influence on the AIO scores for either androstenone or amyl acetate. Individuals with higher responsiveness to amyl acetate (positive intensity and pleasantness) had significantly higher scores for the Positive Smells factor, with no significant interaction between individual responsiveness and androstenone. Individuals with higher responsiveness to androstenone (positive intensity and negative pleasantness) had significantly higher scores for the negative smell factor, with no significant interaction with individual responsiveness to amyl acetate. The researchers repeated the multiple regression analysis after removing those participants who were anosmic to androstenone. Again, amyl acetate intensity and pleasantness were significantly related to the Positive Smells factor, while androstenone pleasantness (but not intensity) was significantly related to the Negative Smells factor. Finally, the researchers found that those who had rated androstenone as extremely unpleasant (1-2 on the scale) had significantly higher scores on both the Negative Smells factor and the Positive Smells factor than those who had rated androstenone as pleasant (7-9 on the scale).

Key Ideas

- Individuals with a higher positive responsiveness to amyl acetate (both intensity and pleasantness) were more likely to view odors positively in interpersonal contexts.
- ndividuals with a higher responsiveness to androstenone (positive intensity and negative pleasantness) were more likely to use odors to reject individuals in interpersonal contexts.
- Individual difference in the perception to odors significantly impacts human attraction, emotions, and decision-making abilities in interpersonal contexts.

WOMEN'S VOCAL TENDENCIES ARE RELATED TO PERCEIVED ATTRACTIVENESS AND FEMININITY

Feinberg, D. R., Jones, B. C., DeBruine, L. M., Moore, F. R., Law Smith, M. J., Cornwell, R. E., Tiddeman, B. P., Boothroyd, L. G., & Perrett, D. I. (2005). The voice and face of women: One ornament that signals quality? *Evolution and Human Behavior, 26,* 398-408.

Preview

This research described three consecutive studies highlighting how vocal tendencies add to the overall attractiveness of a female. First, facial femininity was found to have a positive relationship with vocal pitch. Second, men found composite, average faces of women with higher voices more attractive than those with lower voices. Finally, attractiveness ratings by both men and women of real women's faces had a positive correlation with vocal pitch.

Description of Study

The current study examined the notion that vocal pitch and facial femininity are positively correlated with estrogen and negatively correlated with testosterone in women. The researchers based this conclusion on the knowledge that estrogen is positively linked with reproductive development, vocal pitch, and the expression of femininity. Thus, if both vocal pitch and facial femininity reflect estrogen levels, then these attributes should be positively correlated with each other. Basically, if a woman has a higher vocal pitch, she should *also* have a higher level of facial femininity. Thus, the first study predicted that, for women, vocal pitch is positively correlated with facial femininity. By the same logic, overall facial attractiveness (of which femininity is a part) should also be positively correlated with vocal pitch. To control for individual variation, two composite faces of women were created in the second study to represent an average level of facial attractiveness, one representing a group of women with a higher voice and one representing a group of women with a lower voice. The second study was based on the prediction that men would prefer the average face derived from the group of women with a higher voice over the average face derived from the other group. The third study predicted the same result, using the natural faces instead of the composite faces. The specific predictions of the studies were:

1. Women's vocal pitch is positively correlated with facial femininity.
2. Women's vocal pitch is positively correlated with facial attractiveness.

Method

In the first study, the researchers recruited 108 participants from two universities. A photograph of each participant was taken and measured for facial femininity, which is connected with such features as a prominent cheekbone, eye size, and the mean height of the eyebrow above the eye. The participants also spoke various vowel sounds into a microphone, which was recorded for analysis of the individual's fundamental frequency, an average of vocal pitch on a scale between 100 and 600 Hz.

The second and third studies used faces of 123 female students at two universities, who had their pictures taken and their voices recorded. Using graphics software, the researchers constructed one face averaging the 39 highest-pitched women and another averaging the 39 lowest-pitched women. The two images were placed on the Internet side by side, where male participants rated the attractiveness of each image on a four-point scale.

Results

As hypothesized, higher vocal pitches were associated with greater perceived femininity and greater perceived attractiveness. The researchers believe that these findings support the notion that several female physiological traits, including vocal traits, facial femininity, and facial attractiveness, all reflect qualities of reproductive and hormonal health. The finding that males preferred the faces of higher-pitched women in both Study 2 and Study 3 supports the evolutionary principle that attractiveness is an adaptive physiological characteristic that helps an individual serve the ultimate goal of reproduction. The researchers caution that, due to the small difference in age among participants, later research should use samples with a larger age gap to ensure that age would not factor into any of these traits' influence on attractiveness and health.

Key Ideas

- For women, vocal pitch is positively correlated with facial femininity.
- Men and women rate the faces of higher-pitched women as more attractive than the faces of lower-pitched women.
- Overall, female attractiveness appears to be interrelated among several different traits, including voice, odor, body shape, and facial attractiveness.

Facial Attractiveness is Correlated with Physical Health

Shackelford, T. K., & Larsen, R. J. (1999). Facial attractiveness and physical health. *Evolution and Human Behavior, 20*, 71-76.

Preview

Researchers have studied the phenomenon of the *halo effect* for years. The halo effect is the perception that someone who is physically attractive also has other positive characteristics, such as being smart and healthy. Few studies have attempted to identify a correlation between physical attractiveness and health, however. This study examined potential links between attraction and several self-reported health measures, such as headaches and nausea. Results indicated that attractive participants displayed greater measures of cardiovascular health than less attractive participants, along with self-reporting fewer instances of headaches or a runny/stuffy nose. The researchers used an evolutionary framework to explain their findings, stating that attractive individuals find it easier to achieve the ultimate goal of survival.

Description of Study

The connection between attractiveness and health is important from a variety of theoretical frameworks. The evolutionary paradigm would argue that attractiveness indicates underlying health markers, whereas a social constructionist would be interested in how society's views on attractiveness would shape how people feel about themselves and how those feelings affect their health.

A wealth of previous research examines the perception (also called the halo effect) that attractiveness is positively related to health. For example, both opposite-sex and same-sex raters view attractive individuals as healthier than less-attractive individuals, and men also perceive that attractive women are more fertile. However, only one previous study examined empirical links between attractiveness and health. That study found no relationship between attractiveness and health at any point during adolescence, early adulthood, and late adulthood. However, that study used a somewhat simplistic measurement for health where medical personnel rated the individual on a 1 to 5 scale based on a clinical examination and medical records. The goal of the current study was to replicate that research, using more specific markers of health, including cardiovascular functions and other self-reported health measures. The study predicted:

1. Facial attractiveness is negatively related to physical symptoms of illness (headaches, runny/stuffy nose, nausea/upset stomach, muscle soreness/cramps, sore throat/cough, backache, jitteriness).
2. Facial attractiveness is positively related to cardiovascular health.

Method

The researchers recruited 100 individuals (66 women, 34 men) from a psychology research course at one of two universities in the midwestern United States. Participants were required to complete a daily diary of several health measures, including headaches, a runny/stuffy nose, nausea/upset stomach, muscle soreness/cramps, a sore throat/cough, backache, or jitteriness. For four weeks, participants checked twice daily which of those symptoms they had experienced. One form was required to be completed toward the midpoint of the individual's day, covering symptoms experienced in the first half, whereas the second form was filled out at bedtime, reporting symptoms experienced in the second half of the day. The researchers then collected the reports on a daily basis. 90% of participants completed 100% of the self-reports. Variables for the seven symptoms were then created by totaling the amount of times a various symptom was reported over the course of the month.

The participants were also measured for cardiovascular health through a cardiac recovery procedure during a lab session. A photoplethysmograph was attached to the thumb of the participant for continuous monitoring of heart rate. For this process, participants first elevated their heart rate through either riding a stationary bike or moving up and down a step for one minute. This small amount of exercise elevated the heart rate at least 30 beats per minute (BPM). The participants were then allowed to relax in a comfortable chair. For individuals who rode the bike, cardiovascular health was assessed by measuring heart rate four minutes after the exercise. For individuals who chose the step, cardiovascular health was assessed by the amount of time it took for the heart rate to return to baseline. Health scores were then standardized for each technique before conducting analysis, a technique common with previous research.

Facial attractiveness was measured through observer ratings of a head-and-shoulders picture of each participant. Observers were an independent group of 37 individuals (18 men and 19 women) from another psychology course. The observers were asked to rate each face on a 9-point scale, where -4 was the least attractive, 4 was the most attractive, and 0 was the midpoint. Another group of 15 raters separately assessed the photos for the level of smiling.

Results

Because both smiling and the individual's activity level could mediate any relationship between facial attractiveness and health, both variables were first assessed and controlled for in the results. Overall, for the entire sample, facial attractiveness was positively related to cardiovascular health and negatively related to self-reported headaches and runny/stuffy noses. When split by sex, the results were stronger for men than for women. Specifically, for men, facial attractiveness was positively correlated with cardiovascular health and negatively correlated with the frequency of runny/stuffy nose and sore throat/cough. For women, facial attractiveness was only negatively correlated with the self-reported amount of headaches.

Although these findings were relatively modest, they begin to show an empirical link between aspects of attractiveness and physical health, consistent with an evolutionary framework. Instead of viewing attractiveness only a social construction, the researchers conclude that there may be a biological foundation that can also provide us key information about health. However, for this particular study, the researchers cautioned that, due to a relatively small sample size, the limited number of physical analyses, and previous conflicting research, more research should be conducted to more properly determine the scope of the relationship between attractiveness and health.

Key Ideas

- Facial attractiveness is positively correlated with cardiovascular health.

- Facial attractiveness is negatively correlated with headaches and runny or stuffy noses.

Chapter Eleven: Parenting

The papers in this final chapter deal with the experience of bearing and raising children. The first two papers deal specifically with fatherhood. Both Gray et al. and Storey et al. studied changes in testosterone level that men experience when they become fathers.

The remaining two papers deal specifically with motherhood. Martorell and Bugental found that stress reactivity influences the relationships between maternal power, children's temperament, and a mother's use of harsh parenting conflict tactics. Finally, Fleming et al. studied the role of cortisol in women's responsiveness to their children.

Marriage and Fatherhood Are Related to Lower Testosterone Levels in Men

---

Gray, P. B., Kahlenberg, S. M., Barrett, E. S., Lipson, S. F., & Ellison, P. T. (2002). Marriage and fatherhood are associated with lower testosterone in males. *Evolution and Human Behavior, 23,* 193-201.

Preview

Salivary testosterone was examined in unmarred men, married men without children, and married men with children. Results indicated that both married men with and without children has significantly lower testosterone than unmarried men. Furthermore, among married men without children, higher levels of "spousal investment" and more time spent with his wife were related to lower testosterone levels. The authors argue that lower testosterone levels among fathers may help facilitate paternal care by decreasing the likelihood that the father will engage in competitive and/or mating behavior.

Description of Study

One important issue for men involves the tradeoff between the time and energy spent in competition and mate attraction (mating effort) and the time and energy spent caring for mates and offspring (parenting effort). Research on nonhuman species indicates that the steroid hormone testosterone is a key mechanism underlying the mating/parenting tradeoff. The *challenge hypothesis* suggests that testosterone facilitates the mating effort and conversely is a hindrance to the parenting effort. Thus, the greater drop in testosterone after becoming married and having children should lead to greater investment in the care for mates and offspring.

In human males little is known about hormones that are related to the mating/parenting effort. Although no study has specifically studied the challenge hypothesis, existing evidence supports the idea that testosterone may mediate the mating/parenting tradeoff. For example, researchers have found that men with higher testosterone were less likely to ever have married and, if they did marry, they were more likely to have extramarital sex. It also appears as though having children can also decrease testosterone levels in men, as researchers found 33% lower testosterone levels in men whose wives had given birth in the previous three weeks as compared with men whose wives were due to give birth in three weeks or less. The goal of this study was to understand the relationship between the mating/parenting tradeoff and testosterone. The specific predictions addressed in this study were:

1. Testosterone levels would be lower in married men than in unmarried men.
2. Testosterone levels would be lowest in married men with children compared married men without children and unmarried men.
3. Marriage duration and male spousal investment would be negatively related to testosterone levels.
4. The level of parental investment would be negatively related to testosterone levels.

Method

The study tested testosterone levels in 58 men (29 unmarried men, 14 married men without children, and 15 married men with children). Participants were asked to collect four saliva samples (two a.m. samples and two p.m. samples), which were tested for levels of testosterone. Participants were instructed to refrain from eating, drinking, smoking, and sexual activity before collecting saliva samples as they can lead to changes in testosterone levels.

A questionnaire was administered that surveyed the demographic, martial, and parenting backgrounds of participants. The questionnaire also contained a stress inventory, a spousal investment measure, and a male parenting effort measure. Moreover, since testosterone levels decrease with age, age was controlled for in all statistical analyses.

Results

For the total group of participants, salivary testosterone levels were lower in the evening samples than in the morning samples. Results indicated that married men without children had lower testosterone levels than unmarried men. In addition, testosterone levels for fathers were lower than testosterone levels for unmarried men, but not significantly lower than level for married men without children. Contrary to predications, the authors found that the duration of marriage and the male parenting effort was not negatively related to testosterone levels. However, spousal investment and time spent with spouses was negatively related to testosterone levels among married men without children.

These results generally support the challenge hypothesis in that testosterone mediates the tradeoff between mating and parenting effort in human males. Thus, testosterone levels are generally higher in unmarried men as they only invest in mating efforts, whereas lower testosterone levels are found in married men with and without children as they must also invest caring for their mates and/or their children.

Key Ideas

- Testosterone facilitates the mating effort but is a hindrance to the parenting effort.
- Testosterone levels are lower in married men with and without children compared to unmarried men.
- Testosterone levels are negatively related to both spousal investment and time men spend with their spouses.

Hormone Levels Change in Men Following the Birth of their Children

---

Storey, A. E., Walsh, C. J., Quinton, R. L., & Wynne-Edwards, K. E. (2000). Hormonal correlates of paternal responsiveness in new and expectant fathers. *Evolution and Human Behavior, 21*, 79-95.

Preview

Researchers know little about the physiological and behavioral changes that expectant fathers go through prior to and after the birth of their babies. Thus, this study examined hormone concentrations in both expectant and new fathers and mothers. Furthermore, changes in hormone levels were examined in response to cues from newborn infants. Men and women had similar differences in hormone levels, with higher concentrations of prolactin and cortisol before the birth of their babies, and lower levels of testosterone and estradiol after birth. Men with more pregnancy (couvade) symptoms and men who were most affected by the infant reactivity test had higher levels of prolactin and greater reductions in testosterone. Furthermore, hormone concentration were generally correlated between marriage partners.

Description of Study

Effective parental care is a critical component of infant survival in humans. Although in many species paternal care is not needed for the survival of offspring, however in humans, paternal care can greatly increase the chances of survival for offspring. In fact, fewer that 10% of mammalian species are naturally paternal, one of which is humans.

Research has demonstrated that the rapid hormone changes in mothers at the birth of their child facilitates maternal behavior, but little is known about hormone changes in fathers.

Generally, men show great variation individually and culturally in the amount of paternal care they provide to their children. Paternal care is often highest when couple intimacy is also high. Furthermore, male pregnancy (couvade) symptoms are more common in cultures with high levels of paternal care and couple intimacy. These types of symptoms may be indicators of the physiological changes that help men prepare for fatherhood. Thus, it is possible that close contact with a pregnant partner can help increase hormonal changes which facilitate paternal care and responsiveness in men. Furthermore, the authors hypothesize that hormone changes promote paternal behavior, but that individual males are different in the social experiences that induce these hormone changes.

Research on other paternal species has shown a relationship between the increase of the hormone prolactin and the onset of paternal care. Furthermore, many times this increase in prolactin occurs around the same time as testosterone levels decrease. Finally, cortisol is found to be higher just prior to birth in paternal species. This consistent hormone change in paternal animals, which is not found in nonpaternal ones, supports the need for investigation of hormone changes in humans.

The specific predictions addressed in this study were:

1. Hormone changes in men start prior to the birth of their children and continue into the postnatal period.
2. Individual variation in hormone levels is related to male pregnancy (couvade) symptoms and to men's responsiveness to infant cues.
3. Situational reactivity to infant cues increase close to birth.

Method

The study tested prolactin, cortisol, and sex hormones (testosterone and estradiol) in 34 couples recruited from prenatal class. Couples provided blood samples at different times either before or after the birth of their babies. Specifically, the sample can be broken into four groups consisting of early and late prenatal (before birth) groups and early and late postnatal (after birth) groups. Three couples were tested both before and after the birth of their children. All of the hormone testing was conducted between 4 p.m. and 8 p.m. so the diurnal rhythms in hormone concentrations would be constant. Furthermore, late afternoon and early evenings are times when these hormone levels are typically low and relatively stable.

Couples also participated in a situational reactivity test which assessed hormone reactivity levels. Specifically, fathers held their newborn child and the mothers held a doll that was wrapped in a blanket worn by their newborn baby in the past 24 hours. They were then exposed to two video clips, one which included newborn babies' cries. Couples then completed a questionnaire on their pregnancy symptoms and response to the baby stimuli (baby cries). Men who had two or more pregnancy symptoms were classified as having couvade syndrome.

Results

There was a significant positive relationship between cortisol and prolactin levels in the early prenatal group for both men and women. Women in the late prenatal group had higher levels of prolactin than women in the other three stages. Moreover, women in the early prenatal group had higher levels of prolactin than women in the late postnatal group. Conversely, there were no differences between the groups for men's levels of prolactin.

Cortisol levels also differed among groups with the highest levels found in the late prenatal groups for both men and women. Additionally, cortisol levels in the early prenatal group were higher for women than either of the postnatal groups.

Sex hormones (estradiol and testosterone) also differed among groups. Women showed the largest changes in estradiol over the four periods as compared to the other hormones. Again estradiol level were at their highest in the late prenatal group as compared to the other three groups. In men, testosterone was lower in the early postnatal group than compared to the late prenatal group.

In the three couples tested both before and after the birth of their child, men showed a decrease in testosterone and women showed a decrease in estradiol from the prenatal to postnatal periods.

In the situational reactivity test, there were significant differences between the samples taken before and after the test. Specifically, decreases were found for both men and women for both prolactin and cortisol. In both men and women higher baseline levels of cortisol were related with great situational reactivity, however this association was much stronger in men than women.

Men who reported feeling concerned in response to the baby cries had higher average levels of prolactin than other men. Moreover, men who felt concerned or wanted to comfort the baby had a greater decrease in testosterone levels in response to the stimuli than other men. Men with two or more pregnancy (couvade) symptoms had higher average prolactin levels than men with fewer than two symptoms. Additionally, men with two or more symptoms showed a greater decrease in testosterone levels in response to the baby cries. Finally, men whose partners reported feeling concerned about the baby cries has a larger cortisol and prolactin response than men whose partner did not report feeling concerned about the baby cries.

Female hormone levels for estradiol, cortisol, and prolactin were all higher as birth approached in prenatal couples. There were no significant changes in men as birth approached.

Key Ideas

- Hormone changes underlie the onset of nurturing behavior in mothers; however, little is know about the hormone changes that new fathers go through.

- Men and women had similar differences in hormone levels, with higher concentrations of prolactin and cortisol before the birth of their babies, and lower levels of testosterone and estradiol after birth.

- Men with more pregnancy (couvade) symptoms and men who were most affected by the infant reactivity test had higher levels of prolactin and greater reductions in testosterone.

CORTISOL REACTIVITY MEDIATES THE RELATIONSHIP BETWEEN BOTH PARENTAL POWER AND A CHILD'S TEMPERAMENT ON HARSH PARENTING CONFLICT TACTICS

Martorell, G. A., & Bugental, D. B. (2006). Maternal variations in stress reactivity: Implications for harsh parenting practices with very young children. *Journal of Family Psychology, 20,* 641-647.

Preview

A large body of research has linked various parental and societal factors to harsh parenting. However, little has been accomplished in understanding the mechanisms of harsh parenting practices. This study proposed the notion of stress reactivity in the form of elevated cortisol as a mediating variable. Mothers filled out several questionnaires that tested the family history of stress, the behavior of their toddlers, their control of their caregiving behaviors, and the amount of harsh caregiving behaviors. Cortisol measures were taken before and after the Strange Situation activity, wherein the toddler is separated from his or her mother. The mother's perceived control over the failure of the toddler moderated the effect of the child's temperament on the mother's cortisol reactivity after the Strange Situation. More important, cortisol reactivity mediated the effect of both the mother's perceived powerlessness and the child's difficult temperament on harsh parenting practices.

Description of Study

Previous research has highlighted the problem of parents that have a "blame-first" attitude toward their children, resulting in higher tendencies of harsh parenting behaviors, especially with those children with more difficult temperaments. Parents also see themselves as powerless victims, with the child as the power broker in the family. This leaves the parent with no choice but to be harsh and strict. Importantly, the perception of a "difficult" child may differ due to the parent's perception of power, as the same child can be deemed unresponsive by one parent and a troublemaker by the other. These parental perceptions of child temperament have been linked to the problem of child abuse. Previous studies have found that mothers with low power are more likely than mothers with high power to abuse their child, and mothers who were told that their children were being disruptive on purpose became angrier and overreacted in their modes of discipline.

However, less has been accomplished in discovering any mediating variable that interacts with this problem. Thus, the researchers proposed that cortisol, as a function of the mother's stress reactivity, would mediate the relationship between the powerlessness of the parent and the temperament of the child with harsh parenting practices. The specific predictions in this study were:

1. The highest levels of cortisol reactivity and use of harsh parenting are experienced by mothers with low perceived power interacting with difficult children.
2. Cortisol reactivity mediates the relationship between the predictor variables of perceived power and child temperament with the use of harsh control tactics.

Method

Researchers recruited sixty mothers (predominantly Mexican-American) of toddlers. The participants were referred by professionals in health-care programs (the mothers were either participants or had been accepted in the programs at the time of the study). The mothers had filled out several self-report measures for the health-care program. The Family Stress Checklist measured the overall stress level of the history of the family, including history of abuse, criminal behavior, or work with child protection services, and was only used as a potential covariate in the study. The amount of power felt by the parent was measured with the Parent Attribution Test, which asks the participant to assess various causes for both successful and unsuccessful caregiving outcomes. Finally, harsh parenting was assessed with the Conflict Tactics Scale, measuring the amount of times parents would use such behaviors as spanking, shoving, slapping, or pushing the child. The only measure mothers were asked to fill out when they came to the lab dealt with the temperament of the child, assessed by the Toddler Behavior Assessment Questionnaire, combining three subscales on the activity of the children, their proneness to anger, and their tendency to express pleasure.

Cortisol measures were taken from the mothers on three occasions: when they entered the lab; following a nonstressful baseline period where the mother and child engaged in a fun activity; and, following the Strange Situation, wherein the child is repeatedly separated from and reunited with the parent. The Strange Situation has long been used in research as a source of stress to both the child and the mother.

Results

The Family Stress Checklist, while correlated to harsh parenting behavior, was uncorrelated with cortisol reactivity, and was therefore not used as a covariate in the study. The powerlessness of the mother also significantly predicted harsh parenting behavior in response to difficult children.

As predicted, the powerlessness of the mother significantly predicted higher amounts of cortisol reactivity in response to the Strange Situation for those with difficult children and not for those with easy children. This supports previous research that parents with lower perceived power view themselves as a victim in a stressful situation involving their child. This, in turn, causes parents to become more aroused, defending themselves against the stressor.

The amount of cortisol reactivity was also found to mediate the relationship between the two predictors of mother/child behavior (powerlessness and temperament) and the use of harsh parenting tactics. This finding adds to the above conclusion in that the parent will turn to harsher conflict tactics in order to defend themselves against the stressor (in this case, the child). Overall, the study leads to the possible conclusion that cortisol reactivity is an important variable to consider when assessing probability for child abuse and parental conflict tactics.

The researchers posit one explanation found in the physiological result of cortisol reactivity. When cortisol levels rise, they cross the blood-brain barrier, activating the brain to the stressful situation. The two parts of the brain most affected by this are the hippocampus and the amygdala. The hippocampus deals with the processing of the relevant information associated with this event, and places it within a certain context. The amygdala helps mediate our responses to anxiety and fear. Thus, it is probable that mothers with low perceived power will place this stressful event in the context of a high-threat situation, and will respond in a harsh fashion as a defense mechanism against the anxiety and fear being created by the event. Importantly, this explanation uses physiological, psychological, and behavioral factors, highlighting the integrative functions of all three elements.

Essentially, the authors claim that the physiological function of stress reactivity, as found in heightened levels of the stress hormone cortisol, directly affects the path of parental powerlessness and child temperament to actual conflict tactics by the parent.

Key Ideas

- Cortisol reactivity predicted the effect of the perceived temperament of the child on the perceived powerlessness of the parent.

- Cortisol reactivity mediated the relationship between both perceived parental powerlessness and the perceived temperament of a child on the usage of harsh parenting techniques.

Cortisol is Related to Maternal Responsiveness in Human Mothers

---

Fleming, A. S., Steiner, M., & Corter, C. (1997). Cortisol, hedonics, and maternal responsiveness in human mothers. *Hormones and Behavior, 32*, 85-98.

Preview

The association between hormones and nurturing behavior from new mothers to their infants is well documented in animals; however, less is known about postpartum hormones and behavior in humans. We do know that new mothers are more attracted to the smell of newborns than are non-mothers. The authors of the current study investigated the relationship between postpartum hormones and the behavioral of maternal responsiveness. New mothers were asked to rate the pleasantness of different odors and complete a questionnaire about their attitudes toward infants, care-taking, maternal adequacy, and their interpersonal relationships. In addition, the mothers were videotaped interacting with their babies after they provided saliva samples to test for concentrations of cortisol, progesterone, and testosterone. Mothers who had higher concentrations of cortisol were better able to recognize and were more attracted to their own baby's body odor. Cortisol was not related to the attitudinal measures; however, mothers who had interacted more with babies in the past had more positive maternal attitudes and were more attracted to infant odors. Prior maternal experience and postpartum cortisol were the most salient predictors of mothers' attraction to infant odors.

Description of Study

Attempts to relate postpartum hormones to maternal attitudes have been unsuccessful; however, when behavior with new infants is considered, there is a different outcome. Previous pilot studies have found a relationship between the stress hormone cortisol and responses to both infant odors and infant cries. Surprisingly, estradiol or progesterone did not have the same effects. Based on these findings, the authors of the current study worked to determine how cortisol affects maternal responsiveness, attitudinally and behaviorally. Levels of progesterone and testosterone were also measured to compare against other measures. The specific prediction addressed in this study was:

1. During the early postpartum period, hormones are related to behavior rather than to cognition or attitudes.

Method

This study was conducted using 63 new mothers who had full-term vaginal deliveries. On the first postpartum day, participants provided odor samples from their infants, including general body odors (e.g., soiled T-shirts) and urine odors. In addition, saliva samples were taken from the mothers 20 minutes before interacting with their infants. On the second day, mothers were asked to rate the pleasantness of five different odors: general infant body odor collected on a T-shirt, infant urine (each collected both from the mother's own infant and from an unfamiliar infant, for a total of four odors), and a control odor of the spice marjoram. After rating each odor for pleasantness, mothers were asked a total of three times which T-shirt belonged to their own infant.

Between days one and two, mothers were asked to fill out the childbirth and attitude questionnaires. The extensive questionnaires took over an hour to complete. In addition to maternal attitudes, the questionnaires included topics such as physical symptoms, moods, baby temperament, feeding habits, demographic information, and background. Mothers also provided saliva samples to test for concentrations of cortisol, progesterone, and testosterone. Finally, mothers were videotaped interacting with their infants for 20 minutes. Behavioral categories included looking at their baby, talking to their baby, having affectionate contact (hugging, stroking), close proximity to their baby, caretaking, and overall activity with the infant.

Results

There was no relationship found between levels of progesterone and any of the outcomes measured; therefore, this hormone was omitted from further analysis. This finding is a result of rapid decrease in progesterone levels after childbirth. Testosterone had some effect on maternal attitude and behavior but was not the focus of the study; rather, the authors focused primarily on cortisol.

When all participants were analyzed together, there was no relationship between the pleasantness ratings of the odorants and cortisol. The same was true for cortisol and maternal behavior, as well as cortisol and recognition of own infants' smell. When mothers were analyzed separately based on their prior experience with infants, however, a different result emerged.

For first-time mothers, cortisol and maternal behavior were related. Among these mothers, those with higher cortisol levels were more affectionate with their infants. More experienced mothers engaged in more caretaking activities than did first-time mothers. This cold be the result of having more experience with giving birth. There was no relationship between maternal attitudes and cortisol for either group.

Prior experience with babies and cortisol levels were associated with pleasantness ratings. First-time mothers with higher cortisol levels were more attracted to infants' body and urine odors than were first-time mothers with lower cortisol levels. There was no such difference for more experienced mothers. Moreover, there was no relationship between hormone levels and mothers' ratings of the spice odor, suggesting that the association between cortisol and attraction to odors is specific to infants.

There was a significant relationship between cortisol and infant recognition with experienced mothers. Those with higher cortisol levels were more accurate at recognizing their own child's odor than were those with lower cortisol levels. Why the stress hormone cortisol has these particular effects on attraction to odors and recognition of infants is still unclear.

Key Ideas

- Mothers' concentrations of cortisol were related to their attraction to infants' body odors and their ability to recognize their own infants' smell.

- Experienced mothers had more positive maternal attitudes and were more attracted to infant odors than were first-time mothers.

- Prior maternal experience and postpartum cortisol were the most salient predictors of mothers' attraction to infant odors.

About the Authors

Kory Floyd is associate professor of human communication and director of the communication sciences laboratory at Arizona State University. He holds a PhD in communication from University of Arizona, an MA in speech from University of Washington, and a BA in English literature from Western Washington University. His research focuses on the communication of affection in families and other personal relationships, and on the associations between communication behaviors and physiological activities. He has received a number of awards for his research, including the Gerald R. Miller Early Career Achievement Award from the International Association for Relationship Research.

Alan Mikkelson is assistant professor of communication studies at Whitworth College. He received his MA and PhD in human communication from Arizona State University and his BA in speech communication and religion from Whitworth College. His current research focuses on the communication of closeness in adult sibling relationships and on the use of nonverbal immediacy in preaching.

Colin Hesse is a doctoral student in human communication at Arizona State University. He received his BA in speech communication and religion from Whitworth College. His work focuses on the emotional discourse of affection and the psychological construct of alexithymia. He currently holds the Jeannie Herberger doctoral fellowship in human communication at Arizona State University.

References

Aboyoun, D. C., & Dabbs, J. M. (1998). The Hess pupil dilation findings: Sex or novelty? *Social Behavior and Personality, 26*, 415-420.

Altemus, M., Deuster, E. G., Carter, C. S., & Gold, P. (1995). Suppression of hypothalamic-pituitary-adrenal axis responses to stress in lactating women. *Journal of Clinical Endocrinology and Metabolism, 80*, 2954-2959.

Amico, J. A., Johnston, J. M., & Vagnucci, A. H. (1994). Suckling induced attenuation of plasma cortisol concentrations in postpartum lactating women. *Endocrinology Research, 20*, 79-87.

Andersen, P. A., Todd-Mancillas, W. R., & DiClemente, L. (1980). The effects of pupil dilation in physical, social, and task attraction. *Australian Scan: Journal of Human Communication, 7 & 8*, 89-95.

Andreassi, J. L. (2000). *Psychophysiology: Human behavior and physiological response* (4th ed.). Mahwah, NJ: Erlbaum.

Archer, J. (1994). Testosterone and aggression. *Journal of Offender Rehabilitation, 5*, 3-25.

Arletti, R., Benelli, A., & Bertolini, A. (1992). Oxytocin involvement in male and female sexual behavior. *Annals of the New York Academy of Sciences, 652*, 180-193.

Bassett, J. R., Marshall, P. M., & Spilane, R. (1987). The physiological markers of acute stress (public speaking) in bank employees. *Psychophysiology, 5*, 265-273.

Baum, A., & Grunberg, N. (1995). Measurement of stress hormones. In S. Cohen, R. C. Kessler, & L. U. Gordon (Eds.), *Measuring stress: A guide for health and social scientists* (pp. 175-192). New York: Oxford University Press.

Beatty, M. J., & McCroskey, J. C. (1997). It's in our nature: Verbal aggressiveness as temperamental expression. *Communication Quarterly, 45*, 446-460.

Beatty, M. J., & McCroskey, J. C. (1998). Interpersonal communication as temperamental expression: A communibiological paradigm. In J. C. McCroskey, J. A. Daly, M. M. Martin, & M. J. Beatty (Eds.), *Communication and personality: Trait perspectives* (pp. 41-67). Cresskill, NJ: Hampton Press.

Beatty, M. J., & McCroskey, J. C. (2000a). A few comments about communibiology and the nature/nurture question. *Communication Education, 49*, 25-28.

Beatty, M. J., & McCroskey, J. C. (2000b). Theory, scientific evidence, and the communibiological paradigm: Reflections of misguided criticism. *Communication Education, 49*, 36-44.

Beatty, M. J., Heisel, A. D., Hall, A. E., Levine, T. R., & La France, B. H. (2002). What can we learn from the study of twins about genetic and environmental influences on interpersonal affiliation, aggressiveness, and social anxiety? A meta-analytic study. *Communication Monographs, 69*, 1-18.

Beatty, M. J., Marshall, L. A., & Rudd, J. E. (2001). A twins study of communicative adaptability: Heritability of individual differences. *Quarterly Journal of Speech, 87*, 366-377.

Beatty, M. J., McCroskey, J. C., & Heisel, A. D. (1998). Communication apprehension as temperamental expression: A communibiological paradigm. *Communication Monographs, 64*, 197-219.

Beatty, M. J., McCroskey, J. C., & Valencic, K. M. (2001). *The biology of communication: A communibiological perspective.* Cresskill, NJ: Hampton Press.

Beatty, M. J., & Valencic, K. M. (2000). Context-based apprenehsion versus planning demands: A communibiological analysis of anticipatory public speaking anxiety. *Communication Education, 49*, 58-71.

Becker, J. B., & Breedlove, S. M. (2002). Introduction to behavioral endocrinology. In J. B. Becker, S. M. Breedlove, D. Crews, & M. M. McCarthy (Eds.), *Behavioral endocrinology* (2nd ed) (pp. 3-38). Cambridge, MA: MIT Press.

Berg, S. J., & Wynne-Edwards, K. E. (2001). Changes in testosterone, cortisol, estradiol levels in men becoming fathers. *Mayo Clinic Proceedings, 76*, 582-592.

Bodary, D. L., & Miller, L. D. (2000). Neurobiological substrates of communicator style. *Communication Education, 49*, 82-98.

Booth, A., & Dabbs, J. M. (1993). Testosterone and men's marriages. *Social Forces, 72*, 463-477.

Brown, P. C., & Smith, T. W. (1992). Social influence, marriage, and the heart: Cardiovascular consequences of interpersonal control in husbands and wives. *Health Psychology, 11*, 88-96.

Carmichael, M. S., Humbert, R., Dixen, J., Palmisano, G., Greenleaf, W., & Davidson, J. M. (1987). Plasma oxytocin increase in the human sexual response. *Journal of Clinical Endocrinology Metabolism, 64*, 27-31.

Carmichael, M. S., Warburton, V. L., Dixen, J., & Davidson, J. M. (1994). Relationships among cardiovascular, muscular, and oxytocin responses during human sexual activity. *Archives of Sexual Behavior, 23*, 59-79.

Carter, C. S. (1992). Oxytocin and sexual behavior. *Neuroscience Biobehavioral Reviews, 16*, 131-144.

Carter, C. S., & Altemus, M. (1997). Integrative functions of lactational hormones in social behavior and stress management. In C. S. Carter, I. I. Lederhendler, & B. Kirkpatrick (Eds.), *The integrative neurobiology of affiliation* (pp. 361-372). New York: Annals of the New York Academy of Sciences.

Cascio, C., Yu, G. Z., Insel, T. R., & Wang, Z. X. (1998). Dopamine D_2 receptor-mediated regulation of partner preferences in female prairie voles. *Social Neuroscience Abstracts, 24,* 372.13.

Chiodera, P., Salvarani, C., Bacchi-Modena, A., Spallanzani, R., Cigarini, C., Alboni, A., Gardini, E., & Coiro, V. (1991). Relationship between plasma profiles of oxytocin and adrenocorticotropin hormones during suckling or breast stimulation in women. *Hormone Research, 35,* 119-123.

Dabbs, J. M. (1997). Testosterone and papillary response to auditory sexual stimuli. *Physiology and Behavior, 62,* 909-912.

Damsma, G., Day, J., & Fibiger, H. C. (1989). Lack of tolerance to nicotine-induced dopamine release in the nucleus accumbens. *European Journal of Pharmacology, 168,* 363-368.

Damsma, G., Pfaus, J. G., Wenkstern, D., Phillips, A. G., & Fibiger, H. C. (1992). Sexual behavior increases dopamine in the nucleus accumbens and striatum of male rats: Comparisons with novelty and locomotion. *Behavioral Neuroscience, 106,* 181-191.

Davis, J. (1984). *Endorphins: New waves in brain chemistry.* Garden City, NY: Dial Press.

Denton, W. H., Burleson, B. R., Hobbs, B. V., Von Stein, M., & Rodriguez, C. P. (2001). Cardiovasular reactivity and initiate/avoid patterns of marital communication: A test of Gottman's psychophysiologic model of marital interaction. *Journal of Behavioral Medicine, 24,* 401-421.

Eichorn, D. (1970). Physiological development. In P. H. Mussen (Ed.), *Carmichael's manual of child psychology* (Vol. 1). New York: Wiley.

Ekman, P., & Friesen, W. V. (1978). *Facial action coding system.* Palo Alto, CA: Consulting Psychologist Press.

Ekman, P., Friesen, W. V., & Tomkins, S. S. (1972). Facial affect scoring technique (FAST): A first validity study. *Semiotica, 3,* 37-58.

Ekman, P., Levenson, R. W., & Friesen, W. V. (1983). Autonomic nervous system activity distinguishes between emotions. *Science, 221,* 1208-1210.

Ellison, P. T., Lipson, S. F., & Meredith, M. D. (1989). Salivary testosterone levels in males from the Ituri forest of Zaïre. *American Journal of Human Biology, 1,* 21-24.

Eysenck, H. J., & Eysenck, M. W. (1985). *Personality and individual differences: A natural science approach.* New York: Plenum.

Fehm-Wolfsdorf, G., Groth, T., Kaiser, A., & Hahlweg, K. (1999). Cortisol responses to marital conflict depend on marital interaction quality. *International Journal of Behavioral Medicine, 6,* 207-227.

Floyd, K., & Mikkelson, A. C. (2003). Effects of brain laterality on decoding accuracy for facial displays of emotion. *Communication Quarterly, 51,* 419-437.

Geen, R. G., & Rakosky, J. J. (1973). Interpretations of observed aggression and their effect on GSR. *Journal of Experimental Research in Personality, 6,* 289-292.

Gorman, M. R., & Lee, T. M. (2002). Hormones and biological rhythms. In J. B. Becker, S. M. Breedlove, D. Crews, & M. M. McCarthy (Eds.), *Behavioral endocrinology* (2nd ed) (pp. 451-494). Cambridge, MA: MIT Press.

Gottman, J. M. (1994). *What predicts divorce? The relationship between marital processes and marital outcomes.* Hillsdale, NJ: Erlbaum.

Gottman, J. M., Levenson, R., & Woodin, E. (2001). Facial expressions during marital conflict. *Journal of Family Communication, 1,* 37-57.

Gray, J. A. (1991). The neuropsychology of temperament. In J. Strelau & A. Angleitner (Eds.), *Explorations in temperament* (pp. 105-128). New York: Plenum.

Gray, P. B., Kahlenberg, S. M., Barrett, E. S., Lipson, S. F., & Ellison, P. T. (2002). Marriage and fatherhood are associated with lower testosterone in males. *Evolution and Human Behavior, 23*, 193-201.

Grossi, G., Åhs, A., & Lundberg, U. (1998). Psychological correlates of salivary cortisol secretion among unemployed men and women. *Integrative Physiological and Behavioral Science, 33*, 249-263.

Grunberg, N. E., & Singer, J. E. (1990). Biochemical measurement. In J. T. Cacioppo & L. G. Tassinary (Eds.), *Principles of psychophysiology: Physical, social, and inferential elements* (pp. 149-176). New York: Cambridge University Press.

Herrera, P., Bourgeois, P., & Hess, U. (1998, September). *Counter mimicry effects as a function of racial attitudes.* Paper presented to Society for Psychophysiological Research, Denver, CO.

Hess, E. H. (1975). The role of pupil size in communication. *Scientific American, 233*, 110-119.

Izard, C. E. (1979). *The Maximally Discriminative Facial Movement Coding System (MAX).* Newark, NJ: University of Delaware Instructional Resource Center.

Izard, C. E., Dougherty, L. M., & Hembree, E. A. (1983). *A system for identifying affect expressions by holistic judgments.* Unpublished manuscript, University of Delaware.

Kiecolt-Glaser, J. K., Malarkey, W. B., Chee, M., Newton, T., Cacioppo, J. T., Mao, H., & Glaser, R. (1993). Negative behavior during marital conflict is associated with immunologic down-regulation. *Psychosomatic Medicine, 55*, 395-409.

Kiecolt-Glaser, J. K., Newton, T., Cacioppo, J. T., MacCallum, R. C., Glaser, R., & Malarkey, W. B. (1996). Marital conflict and endocrine function: Are men really more physiologically affected than women? *Journal of Consulting and Clinical Psychology, 64*, 324-332.

Kirschbaum, C., & Hellhammer, D. H. (1989). Salivary cortisol in psychobiological research: An overview. *Neuropsychobiology, 22*, 150-169.

Kirschbaum, C., & Hellhammer, D. H. (1994). Salivary cortisol in psychoneuroendocrine research: Recent developments and applications. *Psychoneuroendocrinology, 19*, 313-333.

Kring, A. M., & Gordon, A. H. (1998). Sex differences in emotion: Expression, experience, and physiology. *Journal of Personality and Social Psychology, 74*, 686-703.

Larsson, K., & Ahlenius, S. (1986). Masculine sexual behavior and brain monoamines. In M. Segal (Ed.), *Psychopharmacology of sexual disorders* (pp. 15-32). London, England: Libbey.

Lawler, K. A., Wilcox, Z. C., & Anderson, S. F. (1995). Gender differences in patterns of dynamic cardiovascular regulation. *Psychosomatic Medicine, 57*, 357-365.

Le Poire, B. A., & Burgoon, J. K. (1996). Usefulness of differentiating arousal responses within communication theories: Orienting response or defensive arousal within nonverbal theories of expectancy violation. *Communication Monographs, 63*, 208-230.

Levenson, R. W., & Gottman, J. M. (1983). Marital interaction: Physiological linkage and affective exchange. *Journal of Personality and Social Psychology, 45*, 587-597.

Levenson, R. W., & Gottman, J. M. (1985). Physiological and affective predictors of change in relationship satisfaction. *Journal of Personality and Social Psychology, 49*, 85-94.

Levenson, R. W., Ekman, P., & Friesen, W. V. (1990). Voluntary facial action generates emotion-specific ANS activity. *Psychophysiology, 27*, 363-384.

Mazur, A., & Booth, A. (1998). Testosterone and dominance in men. *Behavioral and Brain Sciences, 21*, 353-363.

Mazur, A., & Michalek, J. (1998). Marriage, divorce, male testosterone. *Social Forces, 77*, 315-330.

McEwan, B. (1999). Stress and the brain. In R. Conlan (Ed.), *States of mind: New discoveries about how our brains make us who we are* (pp. 81-102). New York: Wiley.

Miller, G. E., Dopp, J. M., Myers, H. F., Stevens, S. Y., & Fahey, J. L. (1999). Psychosocial predictors of natural killer cell mobilization during marital conflict. *Health Psychology, 18*, 262-271.

Mulac, A. (1989). Men's and women's talk in same-gender and mixed-gender dyads: Power or polemic? *Journal of Language and Social Psychology, 8*, 249-270.

Murphy, J. K., Stoney, C. M., Alpert, B. S., & Walker, S. S. (1995). Gender and ethnicity in children's cardiovascular reactivity: 7 years of study. *Health Psychology, 14*, 48-55.

Murphy, M. R., Checkley, S. A., Seckl, J. R., & Lightman, S. L. (1990). Naloxone inhibits oxytocin release at orgasm in man. *Journal of Clinical Endocrinology and Metabolism, 65*, 1056-1063.

Murphy, M. R., Seckl, J. R., Burton, S., Checkley, S. A., & Lightman, S. L. (1990). Changes in oxytocin and vasopressin secretion during sexual activity in men. *Journal of Clinical Endocrinology and Metabolism, 65*, 738-741.

Navarro, M. A., Juan, L., & Bonnin, M. R. (1986). Salivary testosterone: Relationship to total and free testosterone in serum. *Clinical Chemistry, 32*, 231-232.

Nelson, E. E., & Panksepp, J. (1998). Brain substrates of infant-mother attachment: Contributions of opioids, oxytocin, and norepinephrine. *Neuroscience and Biobehavioral Reviews, 22*, 437-452.

Nelson, R. J. (2000). *An introduction to behavioral endocrinology* (2nd ed.). Sunderland, MA: Sinauer Associates.

Panksepp, J. (1992). Oxytocin effects on emotional processes: Separation distress, social bonding, and relationships to psychiatric disorders. In C. A. Pedersen, J. D. Caldwell, G. F. Jirikowski, & T. R. Insel (Eds.), *Oxytocin in maternal, sexual, and social behaviors* (pp. 243-252). New York: New York Academy of Sciences.

Panksepp, J. (1998). *Affective neuroscience: The foundations of human and animal emotions.* New York: Oxford University Press.

Pfaus, J. G., Damsma, G., Nomikos, G. G., Wenkstern, D., Blaha, C. D., Phillips, A. G., & Fibiger, H. C. (1990). Sexual behavior enhances central dopamine transmission in the male rat. *Brain Research, 530,* 345-348.

Porges, S. W. (1995). Orienting in a defensive world: Mammalian modification of our evolutionary heritage. A polyvagal theory. *Psychophysiology, 32,* 301-318.

Porges, S. W. (1996). Physiological regulations in high-risk infants: A model for assessment and potential intervention. *Development and Psychopathology, 8,* 43-58.

Porges, S. W. (1997). Emotion: An evolutionary by-product of the neural regulation of the autonomic nervous system. In C. S. Carter, I. I. Lederhendler, & B. Kirkpatrick (Eds.), *The integrative neurobiology of affiliation* (pp. 65-82). New York: Annals of the New York Academy of Sciences.

Porges, S. W. (1998). Love: An emergent property of the mammalian autonomic nervous system. *Psychoneuroendocrinology, 23,* 837-861.

Porterfield, S. P. (2001). *Endocrine physiology* (2nd ed). St. Louis, MO: Mosby/Elsevier Science.

Richard, P., Moos, F., & Freund-Mercier, M. J. (1991). Central effects of oxytocin. *Physiological Review, 71,* 331-370.

Richardson, G. S., & Martin, J. B. (1988). Circadian rhythms in neuroendocrinology and immunology: Influence of aging. *Progress in Neuroendocrinology and Immunology, 1,* 16-20.

Samson, H. H., Hodge, C. W., Tolliver, G. A., & Haraguchi, M. (1993). Effect of dopamine agonists and antagonists on ethanol reinforced behavior: The involvement of the nucleus accumbens. *Brain Research Bulletin, 30,* 133-141.

Sapolsky, R. M. (2002). Endocrinology of the stress-response. In J. B. Becker, S. M. Breedlove, D. Crews, & M. M. McCarthy (Eds.), *Behavioral endocrinology* (2nd ed.) (pp. 409-450). Cambridge, MA: MIT.

Sayette, M. A., Cohn, J. F., Wertz, J. M., Perrott, M. A., & Perrott, D. J. (2001). A psychometric evaluation of the Facial Action Coding System for assessing spontaneous expression. *Journal of Nonverbal Behavior, 25,* 167-186.

Sicher, F., Targ, E., Moore, D., & Smith, H. S. (1998). A randomized double-blind study of the effect of distant healing in a population with advanced AIDS. *Western Journal of Medicine, 169,* 356-363.

Smith, T. W., & Brown, P. C. (1991). Cynical hostility, attempts to exert social control, and cardiovascular reactivity in married couples. *Journal of Behavioral Medicine, 14,* 581-592.

Stahl, F., & Dorner, G. (1982). Responses of salivary cortisol levels to situations. *Endocrinology, 80,* 158-162.

Storey, A. E., Walsh, C. J., Quinton, R. L., & Wynne-Edwards, K. E. (2000). Hormonal correlates of paternal responsiveness in new and expectant fathers. *Evolution and Human Behavior, 21,* 79-95.

Taylor, S. E. (2002). *The tending instinct: How nurturing is essential to who we are and how we live.* New York: Times Books.

Thornhill, R., & Palmer, C. T. (2000). *A natural history of rape: Biological bases of sexual coercion.* Cambridge, MA: MIT Press.

Turner, R. A., Altemus, M., Enos, T., Cooper, B., & McGuinness, T. (1999). Preliminary research on plasma oxytocin in normal cycling women: Investigating emotion and interpersonal distress. *Psychiatry, 62*, 97-113.

Uvnäs-Moberg, K. (1998). Oxytocin may mediate the benefits of positive social interaction and emotions. *Psychoneuroendocrinology, 23*, 819-835.

Wiesenfeld, A. R., Malatesta, C. Z., Whitman, P. B., Granrose, L., & Uili, R. (1985). Psychophysiological response of breast- and bottle-feeding mothers to their infants' signals. *Psychophysiology, 22*, 79-86.

Glossary of Terms

Adrenal cortex *ah-dre'nal kor'tex* one of two parts of the adrenal gland; produces mineralocorticoids, glucocorticoids, and sex hormones.

Adrenal glands *ah-dre'nal* hormone-producing glands located above the kidneys; consist of the adrenal cortex and the adrenal medulla.

Adrenal medulla *ah-dre'nal muh-dul'ah* the central part of the adrenal gland.

Adrenocorticotropic hormone (ACTH) *ah-dre'no-kor-ti-ko-tro'pic* a hormone produced by the anterior pituitary gland that affects the activity of the adrenal cortex; it initiates the cortisol stress response.

Androgens *an'dro-jenz* hormones, such as testosterone, that control male secondary sex characteristics; similar to estrogens in females.

Anomalous dominance *ah-nom'uh-less* a pattern of hemispheric dominance in which the right hemisphere dominates for language and logic and the left hemisphere dominates for nonverbal behavior and analogic processing, or else in which the two hemispheres share these functions equally.

Anterior pituitary lobe *an-ter'e-er pi-tu'i-tar"e* the front section of the pituitary gland; it produces several types of hormones, including growth hormone, ACTH, and luteinizing hormone.

Antidiuretic hormone *an"ti-di"yer-eh'tik* a hormone secreted by the posterior pituitary gland that promotes the reabsorption of water by the kidneys; also known as vasopressin.

Arteries *ar'ter-ez* blood vessels that carry oxygen-rich blood away from the heart.

Autonomic nervous system *ah"to-no'mik* a part of the peripheral nervous system that oversees sympathetic and parasympathetic responses.

Behavioral approach system a neurological emotion system that motivates people to engage in rewarding behaviors.

Behavioral inhibition system a neurological emotion system that motivates people to avoid threatening situations.

BPM beats-per-minute; an approach to recording heart rate scores as the number of contractions (beats) observed per 60-second window of time.

Brain stem a part of the brain consisting of the midbrain, pons, and medulla oblongata; also known as the reptilian brain.

Broca's aphasia *bro'kuz ah-fay'zhuh* a condition, caused by damage to Broca's area, characterized by the inability to form grammatically correct sentences.

Broca's area *bro'kuz* an area of the brain, usually located in the frontal lobe of the left hemisphere, that controls language comprehension and the ability to speak.

Capillaries *kap'uh-lar-ez* small blood vessels that carry blood from arteries to organs and tissues.

Cardiac muscles *kar'de-ak* striated muscles, found on the walls of the heart, that control heart contractions.

Catecholamines *kat"uh-ko'le-menz* a class of neurotransmitters that includes epinephrine, norepinephrine, and dopamine.

Central nervous system a system, comprised of the brain and spinal cord, that has primary control over most bodily functions.

Centrifuge *sen'truh-fuj* a circular machine used to spin objects very fast, usually to separate them through centrifugal force.

Cerebellum *ser"uh-bel'um* a part of the brain that coordinates muscle movement, regulates muscle tone, and helps maintain equilibrium.

Cerebral hemispheres *ser-e'bral hem'es-ferz* two parts of the cerebrum, the left hemisphere and the right hemisphere.

Cerebrum *ser-e'brum* the largest part of the brain, consisting of the left and right cerebral hemispheres.

Coiter's muscle *koi'terz* see **corrugator supercilii**.

Communibiology *kuh-mu"ne-bi-al'e-je* a perspective about human communication that gives primary importance to the role of temperament and brain function.

Communication apprehension a trait characterized by excessive shyness and fear of communicative situations, such as public speaking.

Confederate *kun-fed'i-ret* a person in an experiment whom participants believe is also a participant but who is actually working for the experimenter; confederates usually enact some type of manipulation.

Control group a group in an experiment that does not receive the treatment or manipulation; results from this group are compared to those of experimental groups.

Corpus callosum *kor'pus kuh-lah'sum* a set of fibers connecting the left and right cerebral hemispheres.

Corrugator supercilii *kor'i-ga-ter su-per-sil'e* a muscle located over each eye above the orbicularis oculi; instrumental in creating furrows.

Cortisol *kor'tuh-sahl* a glucocorticoid hormone produced by the adrenal cortex in response to stress.

Deterministic fallacy *de-ter"muh-nis'tik fal'uh-se* a mistaken belief that connections between biology and behavior imply that biology controls behavior.

Diastolic blood pressure *di'as-tol"ik* an index of the amount of pressure exerted by blood on the walls of the arteries when the heart is resting (between beats).

Diencephalon *di"en-sef'ah-lon* a part of the brain located at the top of the brain stem; consists of the thalamus, hypothalamus, and epithalamus.

Diurnal rhythm *di-er'nal* a pattern characterized by changing levels of a substance (such as cortisol or melatonin) over a 24-hour period; also known as a circadian rhythm.

Double-blind, placebo-controlled (DBPC) experiment an experimental design in which some participants receive an actual treatment, others receive a placebo, and neither the participants nor the researchers administering the treatment know which group a given participant is in.

Eccrine sweat gland *ek'rin* any of the numerous small gland located on the body surface that produce sweat.

EEG see **electroencephalogram**.

Electroencephalogram *e-lek"tro-en-sef'ah-lo-gram"* a procedure for recording the electrical activity of nerve cells in the brain.

Electromyography *e-lek"tro-mi-ah'gri-fee* a method of recording the electrical impulses produced by muscle movement.

EMG see **electromyography**.

Empirical *im-per'i-kul* derived from observation or experimentation; relying on data rather than theory or intuition.

Empirical support *im-per'i-kul* confirmation of a prediction through valid evidence.

Endocrinologist *en"do-krin-al'uh-jist* a specialist in the functions of the endocrine system.

Epinephrine *ep"e-nef'rin* a catecholamine produced by the adrenal medulla; among other things, it increases heart rate when secreted. Also known as adrenaline.

Epistemology *e-pis-tuh-mol'e-je* a branch of philosophy related to the nature of knowledge.

Epithalamus *ep"e-thal'uh-mus* a part of the diencephalons that houses the pineal gland.

Estradiol *es"truh-di'al* the most potent of the estrogen hormones, produced chiefly by the ovaries.

Estrogens *es'tro-jenz* a class of hormones that stimulate female secondary sex characteristics; similar to androgens in males.

Estrone *es'tron* an estrogen hormone that is similar to, but less potent than, estradiol.

Experimental group a group of participants in an experiment that is exposed to a treatment or manipulation; results from this group are compared to those from the control group.

Extraversion *ex"truh-ver"zhun* a style of temperament characterized by a gregarious, outgoing pattern of communication.

Facial Action Coding System a method, created by Paul Ekman and Wallace Friesen, of coding the movements of facial muscles.

Facial feedback hypothesis a proposal by Paul Ekman that making facial expressions of emotion causes one actually to experience those emotions (i.e., smiling makes one happy).

Falsifiable *fal"se-fi'uh-bel* a property of a prediction wherein it can be proven to be false.

Fight or flight system a neurological emotion system that prompts one either to flee from danger or to fight it.

Finger photoplethysmography *fo"to-ple-thiz-mah'gruh-fee* a method of measuring blood pressure by examining the intensity of light reflected from the skin surface and the red blood cells below.

Fissures *fis'zherz* grooves created by the folds on the surface of the brain.

fMRI see **functional magnetic resonance imaging**.

Follicles *fol'e-kulz* structures in an ovary consisting of a developed egg surrounded by follicle cells.

Follicle-stimulating hormone a hormone secreted by the anterior pituitary gland that simulates the production of ovarian follicles in women and the production of sperm in men.

Frontal lobe the portion of the cerebrum located at the front of the brain.

Frontalis *frun-tal'us* the largest of the facial muscles; it covers the frontal bone of the skull and is responsible, among other things, for the ability to raise one's eyebrows.

Functional magnetic resonance imaging a method of studying brain activity that relies on the increased flow of blood and oxygen to active parts of the brain.

Gland an organ that produces and/or secretes substances, such as hormones, for use in various parts of the body.

Glucocorticoids *glu"ko-kor'ti-koidz* a group of hormones, produced by the adrenal cortex, that increase blood sugar levels and help the body to deal with stress.

Gonads *go'nadz* glands producing sex hormones; ovaries in women and testes in men.

Gray matter an area of the brain and central nervous system containing nerve cell bodies and nerve fibers.

Growth hormone a hormone, produced in the anterior pituitary gland, that stimulates bodily growth.

Gyri *ji're* ridges that cover the outer surface of the cerebrum.

Hormone *hor'mon* chemical messengers produced by endocrine glands; responsible for various effects on body organs or tissues.

Hydrocortisone *hi"dro-kor'ti-zon* see **cortisol**.

Hypothalamus *hi"po-thal'ah-mus* a part of the diencephalon responsible for controlling such functions as temperature, digestion, breathing, and sleep.

IBI inter-beat interval; an approach to recording heart rate scores according to the amount of time between contractions. Faster heart rates produce smaller IBI scores.

Immutability fallacy *im-u-tah-bil'uh-te* a mistaken belief that all characteristics of a person that are biologically related are, therefore, unchangeable.

Indwelling catheter *ka'thuh-ter* a flexible hollow tube inserted by venipuncture to allow for repeated blood draws over a period of time.

Korotkoff sound *kuh-rot'kof* sounds produced from the time previously restricted blood is first allowed to flow again to the time it flows freely enough not to produce sound; used to determine systolic and diastolic blood pressure.

Limbic system *lim'bik* a group of brain structures, including the hippocampus, hypothalamus, and amygdala, that regulates emotion, motivation, olfaction, and related functions.

Luteinizing hormone *lu'te-in"i-zing* a hormone, produced by the anterior pituitary gland, that assists in the maturing of ovarian cells and triggers ovulation.

Macro-coding *mak'ro* an approach to coding behavior that focuses on cataloguing the meanings behind behaviors, rather than the specific behaviors themselves.

Magnetic resonance imaging a method of studying brain activity that relies on the movements of hydrogen proteins in active parts of the brain.

Medulla oblongata *meh-du'lah ob"long-got'ah* a structure located at the bottom of the brain stem that assists in regulating heart rate, blood pressure, breathing, and swallowing.

Melatonin *mel-uh-to'nin* a hormone produced by the pineal gland that regulates sleeping patterns.

Micro-coding *mi'kro* an approach to coding behavior that focuses on cataloguing specific behaviors, rather than their meanings.

Midbrain a part of the brain stem involved in controlling reflex actions, such as blinking, pupil dilation, and eye and ear focus.

Mineralocorticoids *min"er-al-o-kor'ti-koids* a group of hormones, produced by the adrenal cortex, that regulate mineral metabolism and fluid balance.

Mixed dominance a default term characterizing those people who cannot reliably be classified as having either standard or anomalous hemispheric dominance patterns.

MRI see **magnetic resonance imaging**.

Naturalistic fallacy *nat"ur-al-is'tik* a mistaken belief that naturally occurring phenomena are, as a result of being naturally occurring, morally or ethically good.

Neuron *nu'ron* cells of the nervous system that transmit messages throughout the body.

Neuroticism *nu-rot'e-sis"em* a style of temperament characterized by excessive anxiety, insecurity, or worry.

Neurotransmitters chemicals released by neurons that stimulate or inhibit cells to which they bind.

Norepinephrine *nor"ep-e-nef'rin* a catecholamine produced by the adrenal medulla; among other things, it increases blood pressure by constricting the dilation of the arteries. Also known as noradrenaline.

Occipital lobe *ahk-sip'it-al* the portion of the cerebrum located at the back of the head.

Orbicularis oculi *or-bik'u-lar"is ahk'u-le* facial muscles surrounding the eyes; responsible for the abilities to open and close the eyelids.

Orbicularis oris *or-bik'u-lar"is or'is* facial muscles surrounding, and controlling the movement of, the lips.

Ovaries *o'var-ez* female sex organ in which ova (eggs) are produced.

Oxytocin *ahk"se-to'sin* a hormone, produced by the posterior pituitary gland, that stimulates uterine contractions during childbirth and the ejection of milk during breastfeeding; also thought to play a role in romantic and parent-child bonding.

Parasympathetic nervous system *par"ah-sim"pah-thet'ik* one of two parts of the autonomic nervous system; responsible for functions related to relaxation and rest.

Parietal lobe *pah-ri'et-al* the portion of the cerebrum located at the top of the head.

Peripheral nervous system *puh-rif'er-al* the division of the nervous system consisting of the somatic and autonomic nervous systems.

PET see **positron emission tomography**.

Phlebotomist *fluh-bot'em-ist* a health care professional trained to draw and handle blood samples.

Pineal gland *pin-e'al* an endocrine gland responsible for the production of melatonin.

Pituitary gland *pi-tu'i-tar"e* an endocrine gland, consisting of anterior and posterior sections, responsible for the production of several hormones, including growth hormone, ACTH, and vasopressin.

Placebo *plah-se'bo* a substance that looks, feels, smells, and/or tastes like an experimental treatment but which is inactive; used to test the effects of treatments.

Plasma *plaz'muh* a clear, yellowish fluid portion of blood in which blood cells are suspended.

Pons *ponz* a bundle of white matter connecting each side of the cerebellum to the other and to the opposite side of the cerebrum.

Positron-emission tomography *poz'e-tron e-mish'un to-mog'rah-fe* a method of studying brain activity that relies on the activity of radioactively labeled water injected into a person's bloodstream.

Posterior pituitary lobe *pos-ter'e-er pi-tu'i-tar"e* the back section of the pituitary gland; it produces the hormones oxytocin and vasopressin.

Procerus *pro-ser'us* a facial muscle located between the eyebrows, above the nose.

Progesterone *pro-jes'ter-on* a hormone that is responsible, in part, for preparing the uterus for a fertilized egg.

Prolactin *pro-lak'tin* a hormone, produced by the anterior pituitary gland, responsible for stimulating milk production in lactating women.

Psychoticism *si-kot'i-sis-em* a style of temperament characterized by delusions or loss of contact with reality.

Pupillometry *pew-puh-lom'it-re* a class of techniques for measuring pupil dilation and contraction.

Reflexes automatic reactions to a stimulus.

Reptilian brain see **brain stem**.

Reticular formation *re-tik'u-lur* a mass of gray matter located along the brain stem; responsible for the ability to attend to certain sensory cues while ignoring others.

Rival explanations means of explaining a predicted phenomenon that contradict the reasoning leading to the prediction in the first place.

Secondary sex characteristics anatomical features specific to each sex that result from exposure to sex hormones and that are not directly involved in the reproductive process.

Serum *sear'um* watery fluid obtained when separating blood unto its solid and liquid components after it has been allowed to clot.

Sex hormones androgens and estrogens.

Sinistrality *sin"is-tral'it-e* left-handedness; a preference for using the left hand.

Skeletal muscles muscles, generally attached via tendons to bone, that make skeletal movement possible; the only of three types of muscles under voluntary control.

Skin conductance a measure of perspiration that relies on the skin's ability to conduct electricity more efficiently when wet than when dry.

Smooth muscles muscles generally found lining the walls of hollow organs, such as the stomach, bladder, and respiratory passages, as well as in blood vessels.

Somatic nervous system *so-mat'ik* a division of the peripheral nervous system responsible for skeletal muscle movement.

SPAFF see **Specific Affect Coding System**.

Specific Affect Coding System a system developed by John Gottman to code specific emotions from the face, body, and voice.

Sphygmomanometer *sfig"mo-man-ahm'e-ter* an instrument, consisting of a cuff and a pressure gauge, used to measure blood pressure.

Standard dominance a pattern of hemispheric dominance in which the left hemisphere dominates for language and logic and the right hemisphere dominates for nonverbal behavior and analogic processing.

Striated muscles *stri'a-ted* muscles in which the fibers appear as though covered with stripes.

Sulci *sul'ke* shallow grooves separating the gyri in the outer surface of the cerebrum.

Sympathetic nervous system one of two parts of the autonomic nervous system; responsible for functions related to excitation and arousal.

Synapse *sin'aps* points of contact between neurons in the brain.

Systolic blood pressure *sis-tahl'ik* an index of the amount of pressure exerted by blood on the walls of the arteries when the heart is contracting (during beats).

Target cells cells with specific receptor sites to which hormones can bind.

Target organs organs with specific receptor sites to which hormones can bind.

Task-evoked pupillary response a method studying pupil dilation in which a stimulus is presented and pupil reactivity is measured.

Temperament *tem'per-ment* a manner of thinking, behaving, or reacting that is characteristic of an individual.

Temporal lobes *tem'por-al* the portion of the cerebrum located on each side of the head, above the ears.

Tendonitis *ten"dun-i'tis* a medical condition characterized by inflammation of the tendons.

Tendons *ten'dunz* strong, non-elastic fibers connecting skeletal muscles to bones.

Testes *tes'tez* male sex organs responsible for the production of sperm.

Testosterone *tes-tos'ter-on* an androgen hormone responsible for the formation of male secondary sex characteristics.

Thalamus *tha'luh-mis* a mass of gray tissue located in the diencephalon; responsible for relaying sensory information to the cerebrum.

Thermistor probes *thur-mis'ter* electrodes used in the measurement of surface temperatures, such as skin temperature.

Thermoregulation *thur"mo-reg-u-la'shun* the process of maintaining a consistent body temperature.

Thyrotropic hormone *thi"ro-trop'ik* a hormone, produced by the anterior pituitary gland, that regulates activity of the thyroid gland.

Vasopressin *va'zo-pres"in* see **antidiuretic hormone**.

Veins *vanz* blood vessels that carry oxygen-poor blood to the heart.

Venipuncture *ven'e-punk"shur* the practice of puncturing a vein in order to draw blood or administer medication.

Verifiable *ver"e-fi'uh-bel* a property of a prediction wherein it can be proven to be true.

Wernicke's aphasia *wur'nik-ez ah-fay'zhuh* a condition, caused by damage to Wernicke's area, characterized by the inability to create meaningful sentences or expressions.

Wernicke's area *wur'nik-ez* an area of the brain, usually located in upper portion of the left temporal lobe, that affects the ability to interpret spoken and written language.

White matter white substance of the central nervous system.

Zygomaticus major *zi-go-mat'i-kus ma'jer* a facial muscle, running diagonally on either side of the face, responsible for pulling the corners of the lips upward during a smile.

Author Index

Subject Index